D1648270

THE
ORATIONS OF MUHAMMAD
(MAY PEACE BE UPON HIM)
(The Prophet of Islam)

Compiled and Translated
from the Arabic

BY

MUMTAZ-UL-MUHADDETHEEN

MAULANA A.M.G.M. MUHAMMAD UBAIDUL AKBAR

M.A. (GOLD MEDALIST)

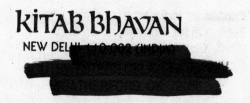

KITAB BHAVAN
NEW DELHI 110 002 (INDIA)

KITAB BHAVAN
1784, Kalan Mahal, Daryaganj
New Delhi - 110 002 (India)
Phones : 3274686, 3263386
Telex : 31-63106 ALI IN

ISBN 81-7151-047-7

Ist Published in India 1979
3rd Revised Edition ... 1991
4th Edition ... 1994

Published by:
Nusrat Ali Nasri for Kitab Bhavan
1784, Kalan Mahal, Daryaganj
New Delhi-110002 (India)

Printed in India at:
Zubin Offset Printers
2090, Guest House
Rod

CONTENTS

INTRODUCTION

The power of speech is one of the greatest or perhaps the greatest of gifts with which man has been endowed. Through the development of this power, not only in the present period, but also in the ancient times, in Greece, in Rome, and also in other countries, the speakers and orators swayed public opinion and secured the leadership of their peoples. To this the Qur'an refers when it says
(He created the man, endowed him with power of expression).

The Arabs attached great importance to their language. "The Arabians," says Hitti, "created or developed no great art of their own. Their artistic nature found expression through one medium only : speech. By virtue of its peculiar structure Arabic lent itself admirably to a terse, trenchant, epigrammatic manner of speech."[1] In Arabia, particularly before the

---

1 *History of the Arabs*, pp 90, 91.

advent of Islam, oratory was considered to be a great
gift, lower only to poetry. An orator was greatly
honcured and respected, at first less than the poet,
but afterwards when the poet degraded himself by
accepting rewards and gifts for his panegyrics and
poems, the orator rose higher in rank to him.[1]

The names of many of the pre-Islamic Arab
orators have been handed down to us by the early
historians and literature. 'Adi b. Zayd al-Abadi,
Khuwaylad b. 'Amr al-Ghatfani al-Ushara b Jabir, Ka'b
b. Luwayy, Ibn 'Ammar al-Tayi, 'Amar b. al-Ahtamm
al-Minqari, al-Zibriqan b. Badr, Suhayi,, b. 'Amr al-
Qarashi are only a few of them who have been
mentioned by al-jahiz in his al-Bayan wal-Tabyin.[2] One
of the most celebrated of them was Quss b. Sa idah,
some of whose orations were attended by Muhammad,
the Prophet of Islam, during the early period of his
life. Some of his orations have been preserved, at
least in parts, by some of the Arabic authors. These
orations represent the model of pre-Islamic Arab
oratory and give us a full view of the picture of the
orations of one of the best pre-Islamic Arab orators, and
of his general style and the method of treatment of the
main topic, followed by him in his speeches. Here is one
specimen of it:

١ايها الناس! اجتمعوا فاسمعوا وعوا ـ من عاش مات ـ و من مات
فات ـ و كل ما هو آت آت ـ و هو القائل : فى هذه آيات محكمات :

---

1. *Al-Bayan wal-Tabyin*, Vol, I, p. 204
2. Vol. I, pp. 53, 65, 275, 276.

مطر و نبات ، وآباء و امهات ، و ذاهب و آت ، و نجوم تمور و بحور
لا تغور ، و سقف مرفوع و مهاد موضوع ، و ليل داج و سماء ذات
ابراج ـ مالى ارى الناس يموتون و يرجعون ؟ ارضوا قا قاموا ام جسوا
فناموا ؟ و هو القائل : يا معشر اياد ! اين ثمود و عاد ؟ و اين الآباء
و الاجداد ؟ اين المعروف الذى لم يشكر ؟ و الظلم الذى لم ينكر ؟
اقسم قس قسما بالله ان لله دينا هو ارضى له من دينكم هذا ـ

"O people: assemble together, hear and remem-
ber. He who lives, dies and he who dies, is gone
for ever. Everything to come is near." (And he said):
"In these things are strong (incontrovertible) signs: rain
and vegetation; fathers and mothers; the passer away
and the newcomer (newly born one); stars which move
and the fathomless oceans; a high roof (sky) and the
ready cradle (the earth) the dark night and the heaven
with zodiac signs. why it is that I see that men die
and do not return? Are they satisfied and therefore
permanently settled or are imprisoned and fell asleep?"
(And he said): "O the people of Iyad! Where are the
Thamud and the Ad? Where are the fathers and
grandfathers? Where are the good deeds for which
no gratitude was shown? And where are the cruelties
against which no protest was made. Quss swears by
God that God has surely a religion which is more
pleasant to Him than the present religion of yours."[1]

It may be noted that the great orator's style

---

1. Al-Bayan wal-Tabyin, Vol. I, p. 247

was simple, free from involved metaphors, and far-fetched similies and ideas, or long introduction. His sentences were short. His method was direct. He drew the attention of his audience to the nature and natural phenomena and the historical events, the memory of which was still green in their mind and just suggested to them his own conclusion. It was cast in the mould of the ideal Arabic composition which has been characterised as   خير الكلام ماقل و دل   —— the best composition is that which is short and suggestive.

This was the model which was followed by the Arabs till the early Umayyad period. All the important Arab orations of this period, which have come down to us, are of this very type having the same general features. The speeches of the early Caliphs, the governors of the provinces and other party leaders are all cast in this very mould.

A Speech of Abu Bakr, the First Caliph

When he was elected as Caliph, he ascended the pulpit and addressed the people saying:

ايها الناس ! قد وليت امركم ولست بخيركم ـ ولكن نزل القرآن
و سن النبى صلعم السنن فعلمنا ـ اعلموا ان اكيس الكيس التقوىٰ ـ
و ان احمق الحمق الفجور ـ وان اقوا كم عندى الضعيف حتى آخذله
يحقه ، وان اضعفكم عندى القوى حتى آخذ منه الحق ـ ايها الناس !
انما انا متبع و لست بمبتدع ـ فان احسنت فاعينونى ، و ان زغت
فقومونى ـ

"O people! I am in charge of your affairs though I am not the best of you. But the Qur'an has been revealed, and the Prophet has created the precedents, and taught us the same and we have learnt them. Know you all that the best wisdom is the piety, and the most foolish thing is to commit sins! To me the strongest of you is the weakest until I regain from him his (the weak man's) right and the weakest of you is the strongest until I regain from him (the strong) the right. O people ! verily I am a follower (of the Prophet's path) and not an innovator (of new principles). So if I do well, help me and if I go astray put me right."

> *A Speech of 'Omar, the Second Caliph, after the confirmation of his nomination as Caliph*

After praising Allah and eulogising the Prophet he said:

فقد ابتليت بكم و ابتليتم بى و خلفت فيكم بعد صاحبى - فمن كان بحضرتنا باشر ناه بانفسنا و مهما غاب عنا ولينا اهل القوة والا مائنة فمن يحسن نزده حسنا ـ و من يسىٴ يغفر الله لنا و لكم ـ

"(O people!) I am inflicted upon you and you are inflicted upon me and I have become a Khalifah among you after my two comrades. We will deal personally with those who will live among us and will appoint a strong and honest man upon those who are absent from us. We will do more good to those of you

who do well and will punish those of you who do evil.
May Allah forgive us and you all."

A Typical Speech of al-Hajjaj
the Umayyad Governor

The whole of Mesopotamia was in rebellion and
al-Hajjaj was appointed as Governor. He had defeated
the rebels at Kufa, and then advanced on al-Basra
where the people were extremely agitated against the
Umayyads and were still in a rebellious state. Al-Hajjaj
went straight to the mosque where people had
assembled for prayer. He ascended the pulpit and
delivered a thundering speech. He said:

ايها الناس ! من اعياه داؤ ، فعندى دواؤ ، و من استطال اجله ،
فعلى ان اعجله ـ و من ثقل عليه رأسه ، وضعت عنه ثقله ـ و من
استطال ماضى عمره ، قصرت عليه باقيه ـ ان للشيطان طيفا، و للسلطان
سيفا ـ فمن سقمت سريرته ، صحت عقوبته ـ و من و ضعه ذلبه ـ رفعه
صلبه ـ و من لم تسعه العافية، لم تضق عنه الهلكة، ـ انى انذر ثم لا
انظر ، واحذر ثم لا اعذر ـ و اتوعد ثم لا اعفو ـ انما افسد كم ولا
لكم ـ ومن استرخى لببه ساؤ ادبه ـ ان الحزم و العزم سلباني سوطى ـ
و ابدلانى به سيفى ـ فقائمه فى يدى ، و نجاده فى عنقى ، و ذبابه قلادة
لمن عصانى ، والله لآمر احذكم ان يخرج من باب من ابواب المسجد
فيخرج من الباب الذى يليه الا ضربت عنقه ـ

"O people! He whose disease has exhausted
him, with me is his remedy. And he whose death
has taken long to overtake him, it is my duty to hasten
it (for him). And he whose head is too heavy for

him, I would remove his burden from him. And he whose past life had been too long for him, I would shorten its remaining portion. Verily the power of the Satan consists in wild thought, and that of Sultan in the sword. The punishment of him who suffers from sickly ideas is just and proper. He who is lowered by his crime is elevated on the cross. He who does not enjoy ample health, the hold of death is not narrow for him. I warn and then I do not wait; I threaten, and then do not accept apology; I admonish and then do not forgive. The mildness of your rulers has spoiled you. He whose girth is loose, his ways are bad. Verily my prudence and resolution have snatched away my whip and have given me the sword instead. Its handle is in my hand, and its suspensory is round my neck, and its fringe is the necklace of him who disobeys me. By Allah any one of whom I command to go out by one door of the mosque if he goes out by another, I will kill him."[1]

These various orations of different orators, of different periods, dealing with different subjects, resemble one another, as one can see, in the general features of style, and method of approach. Their method of approach of the main subject is direct. Their language is easy and flowing. They are free from ambiguity and ornamentation or artificiality, which was the Arab ideal of good speach.[2]

The pre-Islamic Arabs however evolved certain

---

1. *Nihayatul-Adab*, (ed. Egypt), Vol. VII. p. 244.
2. *Al-Bayan*, Vol. I, p. 100

external formalities in respect of their orations. The orators, as a rule, put on a turban while delivering their speeches. They kept a staff, made of wood or iron, or a sword (specially in the battlefields) or a sceptre or a bow or an arrow in their hands. They always delivered their speeches standing (except in the case of marriage orations.) They took their stand at an elevated place, either in the form of a previously prepared stage or on the back of a camel. Seldom they quoted any poem in their long orations.[1]

*　　*　　*

All the Prophets, it appears, needed the help of this persuasive art. They wanted to persuade people to believe and act according to the principles and ideals preached by them. They never employed force for the purpose.

As a matter of fact, few of them possessed it. The only instrument they could use was the sincere and persuasive eloquence. We find a knot' from his tongue (و ا حلل عقدة من لسانى) Qur'an). One may not be, therefore, wrong if he thinks that all the important and successful Prophets were endowed by nature with oratorical gifts.

The Arabs claimed to be the most eloquent nation of the world and called other nations 'ajam

---

1. *Al-Bayan*. Vol. I, pp. 85, III, 196, and Vol. III, pp. 5, 6.

(عجم) i.e., dumb. And among them two tribes were specially distinguished in this respect, viz., the Quraish and the Hawazin. Muhammad, the Prophet, belonged to the tribe of the Quraish by birth, and in the Hawazin he passed his early childhood. Once for the sake of thanks-giving to Allah, he said: 'I am the most eloquent of the Arabs'. On another occasion he said: 'I am the most eloquent among you. I belong to the Quraish by birth and my tongue is the tongue of Banu Sa'd (a branch of Hawazin.''[1]. Over and above his natural aptitude which had been further developed under the influence of his family and society, he is believed to have been specially helped in this respect by Allah. He said: 'I have been sent by Allah with comprehensive pregnant expressions(جوامع الكلم).

During the 23 years of his prophetic career he delivered a large number of speeches which have been preserved in fragments, by historians, biographers and traditionists. But no attempt appears to have been made to collect them together in a systematic form. Their importance, however, cannot be minimised. For they not only represent an important form of speech of the Arabs of the period, but also are expected to throw light on the various historical and religious subjects with which they deal.

Throughout his prophetic life, in his talks and actions of his daily life, the Prophet preached and laid stress on the 'Unity of Allah' and His omnipotence,

---

1 Shibli, Sirat-un-Nabi,. Vol. II, p. 233.

and tried with earnest zeal to concentrate the minds of the people on it. It found its fullest expression in his orations. The principles of Islam formed the burden of all of his orations. He delivered orations in order to give general instructions, to encourage the Muslims in battlefields, to settle a dispute between the two parties, to remove misunderstandings among the Muslims. The main topics of his speeches, however, were moral, religious and spiritual development of humanity.

In the external formalities almost always he followed the pre-Islamic established customs which have been already described. But so far as internal formalities are concerned he introduced certain new features. He always saluted his audience before he began his speech, and the speech itself he always began with the praise of Allah and the two *kalimas* of Shahadah, and concluded with the expression of his wish for the peace of his audience and prayer to Allah for forgiveness.

In the days of festival he addressed the women separately after having addressed the men, and generally urged them on giving alms. Sometimes he stood up to deliver a sermon and contented himself with the recital of a chapter from the Qur'an. Often he recited the chapter 'Qaf' in his Friday sermons and now and then other Suras. In his orations he frequently used to say, more or less, the following sentences:

"Lo, the best discourse is the Book of Allah. The best guidance is the guidance of Muhammad. The worst thing is the innovation in religion. All innovation in religion is heresy. Everything to come is near and the future is never distant. Whatever is destined must come to pass. Allah does not hasten for the hastiness of anyone. Allah intends something, and men want something else; what Allah intends comes to pass. None can bring near what Allah brings near. Nothing comes to pass but with the will of Allah" and so on.[1]

Usually his addresses were composed of simple sentences. But when he wanted to lay stress on any point he put it in the form of questions and answers and repeated one word or sentence twice or thrice such as the oration (No.15) addressing the Helpers at Je'errana and the orations of the Farewell Pilgrimage (Nos. 25 and 26).

His speeches were ,most effective. This must have been due to the sincerity and seriousness with which he delivered them. For when he spoke his colour changed and his body shivered. Every now and then he closed his fist and opened it. Jabir reports that when the Prophet delivered an oration, his eyes became red, his voice rose high and he was overwhelmed with emotion as if he were warming a tribe against the approach of a hostile army and threatening them of the fear of its arrival saying; 'It is at hand! In the morning or in the evening, it will come down upon you and plunder you.'[2]

---

1. Zad, *Guidance in Oration*.
2. Zad, *Guidance in Oration*

His words were so impressive that sometimes the eyes of his audience were full of tears and often they cried out in loud voice.[1] It was his speeches that removed all blood-feud and tribal clashes between Aus and Khazraj. It was his words which, after all, united the whole of divided Arabia into one powerful Muslim nation under the banner of the Crescent by which within one century the kingdom of Allah stretched its one arm to the shores of Atlantic and France and another arm to India and the borders of China.

He delivered speech whenever he thought it necessary. But certain occasions were fixed for it, such as at Friday service, at the two Festival prayers, the day of the eclipse of the sun or the moon, marriage ceremony, etc. His occasional speeches were, generally, longer than the usual speeches. His expressions like those of the earlier Arab orators were pithy and pregnant. His early orations are, usually short. In the last part of his life (8.11 A.H.) he delivered some long orations, e.g., those on the day of Conquest of Makkah in 8 A.H.; on the occasion of eclipse of the sun in the year 10 A H.; at the farewell Pilgrimage, and his last oration which he delivered five days before his death. In these orations he discussed many important principles of Islam, specially social ones.

During his oration if anything important occurred he attended to it and then he returned and finished the remaining portion of his speech. Once a poor man,

---

1. Bukhari, 'Adhabul-Qabr.

Sulayk of Ghatfan tribe, entered the mosque while he was asked whether he prayed two rak'ahs before the Friday sermon. He answered in the negative. The Prophet commanded him to perform the prayers and waited on the pulpit until the man finished his prayer. Then he resumed his sermon.[1]

The sermons in Friday service and in the two festivals of the Qurban and the Ramadan were the part and parcel of the Islamic rituals since the Prophet's time and afterwards they played an important role in the political history of Islam. Later on, to mention the name of the ruling sovereign in these orations, though not prescribed, became customary, and the suppression of the name of the ruler exposed the Khatib or the orator to suspicion of rebellion and disobedience. But this type of the oration, with a fixed order from the ruler, introduced by Marwan, had nothing to do with the simple sermons of the early period of Islam.[2]

In this thesis I have tried my level best to arrange those orations of the Prophet of which at least the approximate dates are known, and so far as possible I have put them in chronological order. It is an extremely difficult task to put together the different portions of an oration, scattered in different places and books, and to present it in a complete and coherent form. Though the subject is wide and the time at my disposal

---

1. Zad, *Guidance in Oration.*
2. *Ency. of Islam*, Khutba.

was short, I believe, I have been able, at least to some extent, to surmount this difficulty.

First I gathered all the different parts, within my reach, which seemed to me to belong to a particular oration: then I searched out almost all the important works, and the different versions of an oration contained in them very carefully, and arranged them according to their sequence of ideas, and put them in their proper places. In many cases the arrangement of the various parts of an oration, to some extent, has been done by me. In some cases I have relied upon the order given by several later authorities like Ibnu'l-Qayyim and Ibnu'l-Hazam and others. But it may be noted that in no case have I added a word or a letter which I did not find in any book the reference of which has been given. Some words of various narrations, of course, are set aside which I could not harmonise, and in such cases I tried to see that my arrangement conforms with that of other authorities the references to which have been given in the proper place. In case the different sources differ as to the context and the idea, I have followed the more reliable and better accepted authorities. But in certain cases I have followed the less weighty works; because they contain more systematic and complete version of an oration. I have entirely omitted the chains of narrations (Isnad and also dropped all sentences which did not form a part of the main discourse, e.g., the questions put by the audience and their answers, etc.

As for the English translation I have tried to make it as literal as possible provided the main import was not affected. My own additions I have always put within brackets. The words 'Amma Ba'du' I have rendered as 'Now to proceed', or Well or As for next or 'Now after', as it has been done by some orientalists.

The following works have been used as sources for the orations included in the present work, and have been referred to in the footnotes by the following abbreviations:

(1)	Sahihu'l-Bukhari, edited by Ahmad 'Ali Saharanpuri	...	Bukhari
(2)	Sahihul-Muslim with the commentary of Imam Nawawi	...	Muslim
(3)	Jame al-Tirmidhi	...	Nirmidhi
(4)	Sunan al-Nasa'l	...	Nasa'l
(5)	Sunan Abi Da'ud	...	Abu Da'ud
(6)	Sunan Ibn Majah	...	Ibn Majah
(7)	Mishkat-ul-Masabih	...	Mishkat
(8)	'Aunu'l Ma'bud	...	
(9)	Al-Mawahibu'l- Ladunniyyah edited by Mustafa Afendi Shahin	...	Mawahib
(10)	Muatta Imam Malik	...	Muatta
(11)	Zad-ul-Ma'ad edited in Maimaniya Press, Egypt	...	Zad
(12)	Al-Tabaqat by Ibn Sa'd edited by Brill (1909 A.D.) at Leiden	...	Ibn Sa'd

(13) Al-Sirat-un-Nabawiyyah
      by Ibn Hisham, Egypt
      edition   ... Ibn Hisham
(14) Al-Sirat-un-Nabawiyyah
      by al-Zaini, Egypt edition
      (1285)   ... Zaini
(15) Al-Sirat-un-Nabawiyyah by
      al-Halabi, edited by
      Afendi Mustafa at Egypt ... Halabiya
(16) Muntakhabu Kanzil Ummal ... Muntakhab
(17) Al-Targhib-wal-Tarhib,
      Egypt edition   ... Targhib
(18) Al-Bayan-wal-Tabin Jahiz,
      Egypt edition (1932 A.D.) ... Bayan
(19) Sirat-un-Nabi (Urdu) Shibli
      Nu'mani   ... Shibli
(20) Encyclopaedia of Islam
(21) Nihayat-ul-Adab by al-Nuwayri

THE ORATIONS OF MUHAMMAD
THE PROPHET OF ISLAM

In Mecca when the verse of the Qur'an "And warn your nearer relatives" was revealed, the Prophet of Islam ascended the Safa hill and asked the Quraishites to assemble together. When they assembled he delivered the following speech. Most probably it was his first speech.

ارأيتكم ، لو اخبرتكم ان خيلاً بسفح هذا الجبل تريد ان تغير عليكم ، أكنتم مصدقي ؟

What do you think? If I inform you that a cavalry is at the foot of this hill and it wants to make a raid upon you! will you believe me?"

قالوا ـ نعم، أنت عندنا غير متهم و ما جربنا عليك الا صدقاً ـ

"Yes", they said, " You are unsuspected among us and we never experienced from you but truth."

قال "انما مثلي و مثلكم، كمثل رجل رأى العدو فانطلق يربأ أهله فخشي ان يسبقوه فجعل يهتف يا صباحاه فانى نذير لكم بين يدى عذاب شديد ـ

He said, "Verily I and you are like a man who saw
the enemy, so he proceeded to warn his people; but he
feared that the enemy would precede him, and he began
to shout, 'Beware of morning raid". So verily I am a
warner to you in the presence of a severe chastisement."

يا بنى عبدالمطلب ، يا بنى عبد مناف، يا بنى زهرة ـ حتى عدد
الا فخاذ من قريش انى الله امر لى ان انذر عشير تك الا قربين و انى لا
املك لكم من الدنيا منفعة ولا من الاخرة نصيبا الا ان تقولوا : لا
اله الا الله ـ

"O the children of 'Abdu'l-Muttalib, O the children
of 'Abd Manaf, O the children of Zuhrah,--till he counted
the branches of the Quraish--verily Allah has commanded me to warn my near relatives. And verily I
possess for you neither any benefit of this world, nor any
lot of the afterworld unless you say 'There is no god but
Allah'."[1]

In Sahihu'l-Bukhari, pp. 385, 702, and Mishkat, p.
460. Indhar, some words of a khutba are found which
the Holy Prophet delivered after the verse "And warn
your nearer relatives" was revealed. Abu Huraira said
that the Apostle of Allah then stood up and said:

---

1. Ibn Sa'd, Vol.I Pt, I, p. 133 Bukahri, P. 702, Tafsir Mishkat, (Delhi)
p. 460; Indhar.

يا معشر قريش — او كلمة نحوها ـ اشتروا انفسكم ، لا اغني
عنكم من الله شيئاً ـ يا بنى عبد مناف لا اغني عنكم من الله شيئاً ـ يا
عباس ابن عبدالمطلب ، لا اغني عنك من الله شيئاً ـ يا صفية عمة رسول
الله لا اغني عنك من الله شيئاً ـ يا فاطمة بنت محمد ، سليني ماشئت من
مالى لا اغني عنك من الله شيئاً ـ

"O tribe of Quraish,--or a word like it--buy
yourselves, I cannot help you against Allah in the least.
O children of Abd Manaf, I cannot help you against Allah
in the least. O 'Abbas ibn 'Abdu'l-Muttalib, I cannot help
you against Allah in the least. O Safiyyah, (the aunt of
the Apostle of Allah), I cannot help you against Allah in
the least. O Fatimah, (the daughter of Muhammad), ask
me whatever you like of my property, (but) I cannot help
you against Allah in the least."

*No. 2 The following oration was delivered by the
Holy Prophet shortly after the oration of the Safa hill in
Mecca. He invited the Quraishites, entertained them and
after the feast was over he addressed them as follows:*

يا بنى عبدالمطلب ان الله قد بعثني الى الخلق كافة و بعثني
اليكم خاصة فقال 'و انذر عشيرتك الاقربين' و انا ادعو كم الى
كلمتين خفيفتين على اللسان ـ ثقيلتين فى الميزان : شهادة ان لا اله
الا الله و انى رسول الله فمن يجيبني فى هذا الامر و يو ازرني ؟

"O children of 'Abdu'l-Muttalib, verily Allah has
sent me as a messenger to the whole creation in general
and to you in particular. So He has said : 'And warn your
near relatives.' And I invite you to two words which are
very light on the tongue and very weighty in the measure,
i.e., to bear witness that there is no god but Allah and
that I am His Apostle. Who will respond to me and assist
me in the matter?"

قال علي رضي الله عنه : انا يا رسول الله ! قال اجلس ـ ثم اعاد
القول على القوم ثانيا ـ فصمتوا فقام على رض و قال : انا يا رسول الله ـ
قال اجلس ـ ثم اعاد القول على القوم ثالثاً ـ فلم يجبه احد منهم ـ
فقام على رض و قال : انا يا رسول الله ـ قال : اجلس فانت اخى ـ

"I will do, O Apostle of Allah, "said Ali:-- may Allah
be pleased with him! He said; "Sit down, ' Then he again
repeated the same words to the people. But they
remained silent and 'Ali stood up and said; " I will do,
O Apostle of Allah." He (again) said: "Sit down." He then
repeated the same words to them for the third time. But
none of them responded to him. And so 'Ali stood up
and said: " I will do, O Apostle of Allah." He said : "Sit
down; you are my brother."[1]

No. 3. The following oration was delivered by the
Holy Prophet in Mecca before his migration. He called
the Quraish in an assembly and addressed them as
follows:

---

1. Zaini, Vol. I, p. 115.

يا بنى كعب بن لوى انقذوا انفسكم من النار - يا بنى مرة بن
كعب ! انقذوا انفسكم من النار - يا بنى هاشم ! انقذوا انفسكم من
النار - يا بنى عبد شمس ! انقذوا انفسكم من النار : يا بنى عبد مناف !
انقذوا انفسكم من النار - يا بنى زهرة ! انقذوا انفسكم من النار - يا بنى
عبدالمطلب ! انقذوا انفسكم من النار - يا فاطمة انقذى لفسك من
النار - ياصفية عمة هد ! انقذى نفسك من النار - فانى لا املك لكم من
الله شيأ غير ان لكم رحماً سابلها ببلا لها - و فى لفظ - قال فانى لا
املك لكم من الدنيا منفعة ولا من الاخرة نصيباً الا ان تقولو الا اله
الا الله -

"O children of Ka'b bin Luwayy, rescue
yourselves from the Fire. O children of Murra bin Ka'b,
save yourselves from the Fire. O children of Hashim,
liberate yourselves from the Fire. O children of Ab'd
Shams save yourselves from the Fire. O children of
the Abd Manaf, rescue yourselves from the Fire. O
children of Zuhrah, rescue yourselves from the Fire. O
children of 'Abdu'l-Muttalib, liberate yourselves from the
Fire. O Fatimah, save yourselves from the Fire. O
Safiyyah, (the aunt of Muhammad), rescue yourself from
the Fire. For verily I do not possess from Allah any
(special) authority for you. But you have certainly got the
right of blood-relation which I shall soon make moistened
by means of its moisture." According to another version,
he said: 'I possess for you neither any benefit of this
world nor any lot of the next world unless you say':

"There is no god but Allah."[1]

No. 4. According to Ibn Hajar of Asqalan and Ibn Hazam of Cordova the following oration was the first oration delivered by the Holy Prophet in Madina on Friday in the mosque of Banu Salim while on his way from Quba to Madina proper in 1 A.H.:

الحمد لله احمده و استعينه و استغفره و استهديه و اومن به و لا اكفره و اعادى من يكفره و اشهد ان لا اله الا الله وحده لا شريك له و اشهد ان محمد عبده و رسوله - ارسله بالهدى و دين الحق و النور و الموعظة على فترة من الرسل و قلة عن العلم و ضلالة من الناس - و القطاع من الزمان ـ و دنو من الساعة، و قرب من الاجل - من يطع الله و رسوله فقد رشد و من يعصهما فقد غوى و فرط و ضل ضلا لا بعيدا ـ

Praise be to Allah; I praise Him; I beg for His help, His forgiveness and His guidance. I have faith in Him. I do not disbelieve in Him. I bear witness that there is no god but Allah, alone, having no partner; and I bear witness that Muhammad is His servant and His Apostle. He sent him with proper guidance, true faith, light and exhortation on account of an interval among the Apostles, want of true knowledge, deviation of the people from the right path, passing of the time, closeness of the Hour (of resurrection), and nearness of the appointed time. He who obeys Allah and His Apostle is rightly guided and he who disobeys

---

1. Mishkat, p. 460, Indhar from Muslim; Zaini, Vol. I, p. 114

them is misled, forsaken and gone astray, far away.

او صيكم بتقوى الله ـ فاله خير ما اوصى به المسلم المسلم ان
يحضه على الآخرة ـ ان يأمر بتقوى الله فاحذروا ما حذر كم الله
بنفسه ـ ولا افضل من ذلك لصيحة ولا افضل من ذلك ذكرا ـ فان
تقوى الله لمن عمل به على وجل و مخافة من ربه عون صدق على
ما تبغون من امر الآخرة ـ و من يصل الذى بينه و بين الله من
امره فى السر و العلانية لا ينوى به الا وجهالله يكن له ذكرا فى عاجل
امره و ذخراً فيما بعد الموت حين يفتقر المرء الى ماقدم و ماكان
مما سوا ذلك يود لو ان بينه آمداً بعيداً و يحذركم الله نفسه و الله
رؤوف بالعباد ـ

"I recommend to you the fear of Allah. For the best recommendation which a Muslim may make to the other Muslim is to urge him to (keep in mind) the next life, and to commend him the fear of Allah. So refrain from what Allah Himself warned you to refrain from. No admonition is more excellent than this and no remembrance is better than this. Surely the fear of Allah, for him who acts accordingly with a fearful caution and dread of his Lord, is true help to attain what you desire of the affair of the next world. He who joins what is between him and between Allah, secretly as well as openly, desiring hereby nothing but the pleasure of Allah, will gain for himself fame in the near future and a treasure for the life after death when man will need whatever he previously stored up, and will prefer to be far away from everything else. Allah cautions you about

Himself and Allah is very compassionate to His slaves."

هو الذى صدق قوله و انجز وعده، لا خلاف لذلك و الله يقول
((ما يبدل القول لدى و ما انا بظلام للعبيد ـ فاتقوا الله فى عاجل
امركم واجله فى السر و العلانية فانه من يتق الله يكفر عنه سيأته
و يعظم له اجراً و من يتق الله فقد فاز فوزاً عظيما و ان تقوى الله
توق مقته و توق عقوبته و سخطه و ان تقوى الله تبيض الوجه و ترضى
الرب و ترفع الدرجة فخذوا بحظكم و لا تفرطوا فى جنب الله ـ فقد
علمكم بكتا به و نهج لكم سبيله ليعلم الذين صدقوا و يعلم الكاذبين ـ

"He is the One whose words are very true and
Who fulfils His promise; there is no change for it and
verily He says: ' The word is not altered to Me and
I am not a great oppressor to the slaves.' So fear
Allah in your present and future affairs in secret as
well as in the open. For he who fears Allah, Allah
will forgive his sins and magnify his reward. He who
fears Allah, will receive a great success. Verily the
fear of Allah will save you from His hatred and will
keep you away from his punishment and wrath. And
verily the fear of Allah brightens the face, satisfies
the Lord and elevates the position. So take your share
and do not transgress in the region of Allah of which
He has certainly taught you by means of His Book
and has prepared for you the way leading to Him;
so that He may know those who are sincerely truthful
and also those who are insincere."

فآحسنوا كما احسن الله اليكم و عادوا اعداءه و جاهدوا فى الله
حق جهاده ـ هو اجتبا كم و سما كم المسلمين ـ ليهلك من هلك عن
بينة ـ ولا حول ولا قوة الا بالله ، ويحيى من حيى عن بينة ـ ولا حول
ولا قوة الا بالله ـ

" Do, therefore, good as Allah has done good
to you, be at enmity with His enemies and wage
the Holy War in (the way of) Allah as it should be done.
It is He Who has chosen you and named you Muslims;
so that those who are to perish may perish after the clear
sign (had been given)--there is neither any turn nor any
power except with Allah,--and that those who are to live
after the clear sign (had been given). There is no turn
and no power except with Allah".

فا كثر و اذكروا الله واعملوا لما بعدالموت فانه من يصلح ما بينه
و بين الله يكفه ما بينه و بين الناس ذلك بان الله يقضى على الناس ولا
يملكون منه ـ الله اكبر و لا حول و لا قوة الا بالله العلى العظيم ——

"So frequent the remembrance of Allah and act for
what is to come after death. Because he who repairs
what is between him and between Allah , He will suffice
him in what is between him and between the people.
It is because Allah executes His authority upon the
people and they do not have any power on Him. Allah
is the Great; and there is no turn to and no power with

except Allah, the High, the Magnificient."[1]

No. 5. The following was the first of the orations delivered by the Holy Prophet at the mosque of Madina on Friday, 1 A.H.:

حمد الله و اثنى عليه بما هو اهله، ثم قال : اما بعد، ايها الناس، فقد موا لا نفسكم ، تعلدن والله ليصبعقن احد كم ثم ليدعن غنمه ليس لهاراع ـ ثم ليقولن له ربه و ليس له ترجمان ولا حاجب يحجبه دونه الم يانك رسولى فبلغك ؟ و اتهتك ما لا و افضلت عليك فما قدمت لنفسك ؟

"(The Holy Prophet) praised Allah and thanked Him according to what is due to Him; then he said: Now to proceed, O people, make provision for yourselves in advance. You should know, by Allah, everyone of you will, indeed, faint, then he will leave his cattle without a shepherd. Then his Lord will say to him--while there will be neither any dragoman at hand nor any shelter to hide him--'Did My apostle not approach you and deliver My message to you. I bestowed wealth and favour upon you. What provision did you then make for yourself?

فلينظرن يمينا و شمالا ، فلا يرى شياً ثم لينظرن قدامه فلا يرى غير جهنم ـ

"So he will certainly look to the right and to the left but he will find nothing (to help him). Then he will cast his glance to his front but will see only hell-fire."

فمن استطاع ان يتقى بوجهه من النار و لو بشق تمرة فليفعل و من لم يجد فيكلمة طيبة ، فان بها تجزى الحسنة عشر امثالها الى سبع مائة ضعف ـ و السلام عليكم و على رسول الله و رحمة الله و بركاته .

"So he who is able to save his face from Fire, though by means of a bit of date, should certainly do that; and he who does not afford it then (do it) by means of a good word. For the good action will be rewarded and increased from ten to seven hundred times. Peace be upon you and upon the Apostle of Allah and the mercy of Allah and His blessings."[1]

No. 6. The following oration was delivered by the Apostle of Allah at the battle Badr of 17 Ramadan, 2 A.H. Having praised Allah and thanking Him he said:

اما بعد ، فانى احثكم على ما حثكم الله عز و جل و انها كم عما فها كم الله عنه ، فانه جل و علا عظيم شانه يأمر الحق و يحب الصدق و يعطى على الخير اهله اعلى مناز لهم عنده ، به يذكرون و به يتفاضلون ـ

"Now to proceed, verily I urge you on what Allah,-- the Exalted and the Great,--has urged you on and I forbid you what Allah has forbidden you. For He,--the Great,

---

1. Zad, Vol. I, p. 101. Ibn Hisham, Vol. I. p. 277

High and Magnificent as He is,--commands to do the
right and loves the truth and gives the good men on their
good deeds the highest ranks. He has near Him. By their
good deed they are remembered and on account of it
they excel one another."

و انكم قد اصبحتم بمنزل من منازل الحق لا يقبل الله فيه من احد
الا ما ابتغى فيه و جهه ۔ ان الصبر فى مواطن الباس مما يفرج الله عز
و جل به الهم و ينجى به من الغم و تدر كون النجاة فى الاخرة ۔

'Verily you are now at one of the various stages
of the truth in which Allah does not accept anything
from anyone but that by which His pleasure is sought.
Verily patience in the battlefields is one of the qualities
by which Allah,--the Powerful and the Great.--removes
the calamity and releases from the grief; and (thereby)
you will attain salvation in after-life."

فيكم نبى الله يحذركم و يامركم ۔ فاستحيوا اليوم ان يطلع الله
تعالى على شيئ من امركم يمقتكم ۔ فانه تعالى يقول : 'لمقت الله
اكبر من مقتكم انفسكم ۔

"In the midst of you is the Prophet of Allah
who warns you and gives you command. So feel
(sincerely) ashamed today that Allah the Exalted may
know anything of you, which He dislikes and hates.
For, verily He--the Exalted,--says: The disliking (and
hatred) of Allah is greater than your hatred among
yourselves".

انظروا الذى امركم به من كتابه و اراكم من آياته و اعزكم
بعد الذلة فاستمسكوا به، يرض ربكم عنكم - واسئلوا ربكم فى هذا
الموطن امرا تستو جبوا الذى وعدكم به من رحمة و مغفرة - فان
وعده حق و قوله صدق، و عقابه شديد - و انما انا و انتم بالله الحى
القيوم الذى اليه لجأنا و به اعتصمنا و عليه توكلنا و اليه المصير -
يغفر الله لنا و للمسلمين -

"Look at what He commanded you with in His
Book and at what He showed you of His signs and
gave you honour after you were disgraced. So hold
it; Allah will be pleased with you and ask your Lord
in this field that by which you may deserve what He
has promised you, i.e., mercy and forgiveness. For
verily His promise is true; His word is right and His
punishment is severe. I and you are, indeed, with
Allah, the Alive and Self-existing, of Whom we seek
protection, by Whom we protect ourselves, upon Whom
we depend and to Whom we finally return . May Allah
pardon us and Muslims."[1]

No. 7. *The following oration was delivered by the
Prophet of Islam on return to Madina in Sha'ban 5 A.H.
after the battle of Banu Mustaliq about his wife
'Ae'shah--may Allah be pleased with her:*

عن عائشة رضى الله عنها قالت : لما ذكر من شانى الذى ذكر،
و ما علمت به قال رسول الله صلى الله عليه وسلم فى خطيبا فتشهد
فحمد الله و اثنى عليه بما هو اهله ثم قال :

---

1. *Siratu'l-Halablya*, p. 172 *et seq.*

"It is reported from 'Ae'shah--may Allah be
pleased with her! She said: When was said about me
what was said, while I knew nothing of them, the Apostle
of Allah stood up as   speaker concerning me and
uttered shahada, praised Allah and glorified Him
according to what is due to Him.Then he said:"

اما بعد، يا معشر المسلمين ! من يعذرني من رجل قد بلغني عنه اذاه
فى اهلى ؟ و اثـنروا على فى اناس ابنوا اهلى ـ والله ما علمت على
اهلى من سوء قط ـ و الله ما علمت على اهلى الا خيرا ـ و اقد ذكروا
رجلا ما علمت عليه الا خيرا وما علمت عليه من سوء قط ـ ولا دخل
بيتى قط الا و انا حاضر ولا غبت فى سفر الا غاب معى ـ

"Now to proceed, O community of Muslims! who
will defend me against a man who has caused pain to
me concerning my wife? And advise me about persons
who accused my wife (falsely). By Allah, I never knew
anything wrong in my wife. By Allah, I am not aware of
anything with regard to her but good. They mentioned
a man of whom I know not but good and never knew
any evil of him. He never entered my house but I was
present; nor did I ever go out on a journey, but he also
went out with me."[1]

---

1. Bukhari, p. 595, Iik; Tirmidhi. Tafsir, Ifk

No. 8. *On the same occasion the Holy Prophet went to Ae'shah and delivered the following brief speech to her at the house of Abu Bakr.*

حمد الله و اثنى عليه بما هو اهله، ثم قال : اما بعد، يا عائشة !
فانه بلغنى عنك كذا و كذا، فان كنت بريئة فسيبرئك الله، وان كنت
لممت بذنب، فاستغفرى الله و توبى اليه، فان العبد اذا اعترف ثم تاب،
تاب الله عليه ۔

He praised Allah and glorified Him duly; then said: "Now to proceed, O' Ae'shah there has reached to me such and such (report) concerning you, If you are innocent, then Allah will acquit you and if you have committed a sin then seek pardon of Allah and turn to Him.

Verily when the servant admits and repents, Allah forgives him,"[1]

No. 9. *The following oration was delivered by the Holy Prophet after the conquest of Khaibar in the month of Muharram, 7. A.H when some people of Khaibar complained to him against Muslims that they oppressed the people of Khaibar. So the Holy Prophet stood up and said:*

ايحسب احدكم متكئاً على ار يكته قد يظن ان الله لم يحرم شيئاً
الا ما فى هذا القران ؟ الا و انى قد و عظت وامرت و نهيت عن اشياء،
انها لمثل القران او اكثر ۔

---

1. Bukhari, p. 595; Tirmidhi, Tafsir, Ifk.

"Does any of you think, learning to his seat,
that, as he believes, Allah did not forbid anything
except what is in this Qur'an? Behold, I have
admonished, commanded and forbidden many things.
They are indeed, equal to the Qur'an or even more"

وان الله تعالى لم يحل لكم ان تد خلوا بيوت اهل الكتاب الا
باذن، ولا ضرب نسائهم ولا اكل ثمار هم اذا اعطو كم الذى عليهم ۔

"Verily Allah, the Exalted, neither made it lawful
for you to enter the houses of the people of Scriptures
except with their permission, nor to beat their women,
nor to eat their fruits, if they paid to you their dues.[1]

No. 10. *The following oration was delivered by the
Holy Prophet on the pulpit of the mosque of Madina
when the battle was going on at Muta, in Syria in the
month of Jumada 1, 8 A.H.*

(خطب النبى صلى الله عليه وسلم) فقال : اخذ الراية زيد
فاصيب، ثم احذها جعفر فاصيب، ثم اخذها عبدالله بن رواحة فاصيب،
ثم اخذها خالد ين الوليد عن غير امرة فتح له، و قال : ما يسرنا انهم
عندنا، او قال : ما يسر هم انهم عندنا، و عيناه تذر فان ۔

---

1. Abu Da'ud with 'Aunu'l-Ma'bud, (ed. Delhi), Vol. III, p.
135; Mishkat, (ed. Delhi), p. 29.

He said: " Zaid has taken over the banner and is afflicted. Then Ja'far has taken it up; so he is afflicted. Then 'Abdullah ibn Rawaha has taken it up; so he is afflicted. Then Khalid ibn Walid has taken it up without being appointed as a commander. So he has become victorious." And he said: "It would not be pleasing to us were they with us." Or he said: "It would not be pleasing to them were they with us." And his two eyes were shedding tears.[1]

No. 11. *The following oration was delivered by the Holy Prophet on that Friday on which Mecca was conquered in Ramadan, 8 A.H. (January 530 A.D.):*

قام على باب الكعبة فحمد الله و اثنى عليه فكبر ثلثا ثم قال :
لااله الا الله وحده، صدق وعده و نصر عبده، و هزم الا حزاب وحده ۔

The Holy Prophet stood up on the door of Ka'bah, praised Allah, thanked Him and said "Allah-u-Akbar" three times. Then he addressed:

There is no god but Allah alone. He fulfilled His promise, gave victory to His servant; and He Himself alone vanquished the (enemy) troops.

---

1. Bukhari, pp. 392, 611. According to Ibnu'l-Qayyim (Zad, Vol I. p 416) the battle of Muta took place four months before the conquest of Mecca.

الا ان كل مأثرة فى الجاهلية تذكر و قدعى من دم او مال تحت
قدمى الا ما كان من سقاية الحاج وسدانة البيت، الا انى قد امضيتهما
لاهلهما كما كان ـ

"Behold, that all causes of glory mentioned and
claim as such in the Age of Ignorance, regarding blood
or property, are under my two feet except the services
of water-supply for the pilgrims and chamberlainship
of the House (Ka'bah). Be aware that I let them both
remain under the same persons as it was before."

الا ان دية الخطأء شبه العمد ما كان بالسوط و العصا مائة من
الا بل، منها اربعون فى بطونها اولادها ـ

"Lo, the blood-money for a manslaughter resem-
bling murder, that occurs by a whip or a staff, is
hundred she-camels, forty of which must have their
youngs in the wombs (i.e. pregnant)."

الناس، انه لا حلف فى الاسلام، وما كان من حلف فى الجاهلية فان
الاسلام لا يزيده الا شدة، المومنون يد على من سواهم، يحير عليهم
ادناهم، و يرد عليهم اقصاهم و يرد سراياهم على قعيدتهم ـ

"O people! there is no alliance (on tribal basis) in
Islam. Any such covenant that existed in the Days of
Ignorance, Islam does not make it but more forceful. The
believers are one hand against all others: the lowest of

them can give protection (to anyone) on their behalf and
the farthest of them has to respond to their call and the
fighting soldiers are to allot (something) to the sitting
ones."

لا يقتل مؤمن بكافر، دية الكافر نصف دية المسلم ـ لا جلب، ولا
جنب، ولا يؤخذ صدقاتهم الا فى دورهم ـ

"No believer may be killed in exchange for an
unbeliever. The blood-wit of an unbeliever is half of
that of a Muslim. There is neither transportation (of
the contribution to the poor rates from one place to
another) nor alighting (of the collectors) in the distant
places. (But) the poor-rates will be taken only in their
houses."

و فى رواية، قال : دية المعاهد نصف دية الحر ـ

In another version, he said: " The blood-money
of a covenanted non-Muslim is half of that of a free
man (Muslim)."

المرأة ترث من دية زوجها و ماله، و هو يرث من ديتها و ما لها
ما لم يقل احد هما صاحبه، فاذا قتل احد هما صاحبه عمدا لم يرث من
ديته و ما له شيأ ـ و ان قتل احد هما صاحبه خطأ ورث من ماله و لم
يرث من ديته ـ

"The woman will inherit from the blood-money
of her husband and his property; and he will inherit
from her blood-money and property; as long as one of

them does not kill the other. But if one of them kills the other deliberately, he or she will not inherit anything from his or her bloodmoney and property; and if one of them kills the other by mistake, he or she will be inheritor of his or her property, and not of his or her blood-money.

ولا يتوارث اهل ملتين مختلفتين ـ و لا تنكح المرأة على عمتها ولا على خالتها ـ

"And men of two different religions will not inherit on another. The woman will not marry (co-wife) on her paternal or maternal aunt".

البينة على المدعى، و اليمين على من انكر ـ و لا تسافر المرأة مسيرة ثلثة ايام الا مع ذى رحم محرم ـ و لا صلوة بعد العصر و بعد الصبح ـ و لا يصام يوم الاضحى و يوم الفطر ـ و لا هجرة بعد الفتح ـ

"The proof is to be presented by the plaintiff and oath is to be taken from the defendant. The woman will not journey a three days' distance except with her blood kindred. There is no prayer after the (prayer of) 'Asr (till sunset) and (the prayer of the) morning (till sunrise); and there is no fast on the I'd days of Qurban and Ramadan. And there is no emigration after the Conquest (of Mecca)".

يا معشر قريش ! ان الله اذهب عنكم لخوة الجاهلية و تعظمها بالا بآء ـ و الناس من آدم و آدم من تراب، ثم تلا هذه الاية : يا ايها الناس ! انا خلقنا كم من ذكر وانثى، و جعلنا كم شعوبا و قبائل لتعارفوا، ان اكرمكم عند الله اتقا كم ـ ان الله عليم خبير ـ

"O tribe of the Quraish, verily Allah removed from you the pride of the Age of Ignorance and its ancestral vainglory. Men are the progeny of Adam and Adam came out of earth. Then the Holy Prophet recited this verse: 'O mankind. We have created you out of a male and a female; and We have divided you into nations and tribes; so that you may recognize one another. Verily the more honourable among you to Allah is he who is more pious. Indeed, Allah is All-knowing and Omniscient."

يا معشر قريش، ما ترون انى فاعل بكم ؟ قالوا : خيرا، اخ كريم وابن اخ كريم -

"O tribe of Quraish, what behaviour do you expect from me? They said: (We expect) good; you are a noble brother and the son of a noble brother.

قال : فانى اقول لكم كما قال يوسف لا خوته : لا تشريب عليكم اليوم - يغفر الله لكم وهو ارحم الراحمين، اذهبوا فانتم الطلقاء -

"He said: I say to you what Joseph said to his brothers: 'No reproach is upon you today; may Allah forgive you and He is the most compassionate of the compassionates. Go away; you are free.[1]

No. 12. *The following oration was delivered by the Holy Prophet on the second day of the Conquest of Mecca, Saturday, Ramadan, 8 A.H. (January, 630 A.D.) when the tribe of Khaza'ah killed a non-Muslim of the tribe of Hudhail* :

عن ابي شريح ؟ الخزاعى قال : فقام رسول الله صلى الله عليه وسلم
فينا خطيبا بعد الظهر فحمد الله واثنى عليه ثم قال :

It is narrated from Abu Shuraih al-Khaza'i he said, the Apostle of Allah stood up before us at afternoon as a speaker, so he praised Allah and thanked Him, and said:

يا ايها الناس! ان الله حرم مكة يوم خلق السموات والارض -

"O people, verily Allah made Mecca sacred and inviolable since the day He created the Heavens and the Earth."

ان الله حبس عن مكة الفيل و سلط عليها رسوله والمومنين -

---

1. Abu Da'ud (ed. Cawnpore), p. 269. Diyatu'l-Khata; Ibn Majab, (ed. Delhi), p.192, Diyat; Ibn Majah, (ed Cawnpore), p. 201, Mirath-ul-Qatil; Mishkat, Diyat ; Ibn Sa'd, Vol, II, Pt. I, p. 103; Zad, Vol. I. p. 424; Zaini, Vol. II, p. 111.

"Verily Allah withheld the Elephants from Mecca and empowered his Apostle and the believers over it."

فهى حرام بحر مة الله الى يوم القيامة ـ

So it is sacred and inviolable with inviolability of Allah upto the Day of Resurrection."

فلا يحل لامرىٔ يؤمن بالله و اليوم الاخر ان يسفك فيها دما ولا يعضد فيها شجرا ـ

"Accordingly it is not permissible to any person, who believes in Allah and the Last Day, to shed blood in it and to lop a tree with a hook."

لم تحلل لا حد كان قبلى، ولا تحل لا حد يكون بعدى، ولم تحلل لى الا ساعة من الدهر غضبا على اهلها ـ

"It was never violable for anyone before me; it will not be violable for anyone after me and it was not violable (even) for me except for a little while because of (Allah's) wrath on its people."

الا ثم قد رجعت كحرمتها بالامس ـ لا ينفر صيدها ـ ولا يعضد شوكها ـ ولا يختلى خلاها ولا تحل لقتطها الا لمنشد ..... الا الاذخر، فانه حلال ـ ولا يحل لنا من غنائمها شئى ـ

"Behold, after that it is turned as sacred as it

was yesterday. Its preys will not be sacred; its thorns will not be lopped; its fresh herbs will not be cut off; and its pickings will not be permissible except for the searching officer... excluding the schoenantum. It is, of course, permissible. And nothing of its booties is permissible to us."

فليبلغ الشاهد منكم الغائب ـ فمن قال لكم ان رسول الله (صلى الله عليه وسلم) قاتل فيها فقولوا : ان الله قد احلها لرسوله ولم يحللها لكم ـ

"Those who are present here among you should convey the message to those who are absent. So he who says to you that the Apostle to Allah fought in it, say to him that Allah made it violable for His Apostle and not for you."

يا معشر خزاعة! ارفعوا ايديكم عن القتل ـ فلقد كثر القتل ان نفع ـ ولقد قتلتم قتيلا لا دينه ـ

"O tribe of Khaza'ah, withdraw your hands from murdering. Murdering may be multiplied if it beneficent. You have indeed, killed a man, I shall pay his blood-money."

فمن قتل بعد مقامى هذا فاهله بخير النظرين، ان شاؤ وأ قدم قاتله، و ان شاؤ وأ فعقله ـ

" So he who commits a murder after this stay of

mine here then his people will have option--the better of the two alternatives. If they like they may claim the blood of his murderer and if they like they may take his blood- money."[1]

No.13. *The following oration was delivered by the Holy Prophet in 8 A.H. after the conquest of Mecca when Usama ibn Zaid pleaded to him to excuse Fatimah of Makhzum tribe who committed a theft:*

فلما كان العشى قام رسول الله صلى الله عيله وسلم خطيبا فاثنى
على الله بما هو اهله ثم قال :

" At night, the Messenger of Allah stood up and spoke. He praised Allah with what is due to Him; then he said:

اما بعد، فانما اهلك الناس قبلكم انهم كانوا اذا سرق فيهم
الشريف تركوه، و اذا سرق فيهم الضعيف اقاموا عليه الحد ـ و الذى
نفس محمد بيده لو ان فاطمة بنت محمد سرقت لقطعت يدها ـ

"Now to proceed, verily it destroyed the people before you   that when a noble man among them

---

1. Ibn Hisham with Zad, Vol. II, p. 245; 'Aunu'l-Ma'bud, Vol. II, p. 161; Abu Da'ud (ed. Cawnpore), p. 276; Ibn Sa'd Vol. II, Pt, I, 99; Bukhari, p. 617.

they let him off, and when a weak man committed theft from among them they executed sentence on him. By Him in Whose hand is the soul of Muhammad, had Fatimah, the daughter of Muhammad, committed a theft, I would have cut off her hands."[1]

No. 14. *The following oration was delivered by the Holy Prophet in Shawwal, 8 A.H., when he reached Je'orranah from Hunain and had just lighted from his camel. He stood up among the people and said:*

ادوا الخياط و المخيط فان الغلول عار و نار و شنار على لهله يوم القيامة ثم تنزول من الارض و برة من بعير او شيأ ثم قال : و الذى نفسى بيده، مالى مما افاء الله عليكم و لا مثل هذا الا الخمس، و الخمس مردود عليكم ـ

"Give away (even) the thread and the needle. For the embezzlement is (a matter of) shame, fire and disgrace to its author on the Day of Resurrection." Then he took up from the earth a hair of a camel or something like it and said: " I swear by Him in Whose hand is my soul that nothing from what Allah has given you as booty, nor even a thing like this (referring to the hair) I can get except the one fifth and the one-fifth (also) will be returned to you."[2]

No. 15. *When the Prophet of Islam distributed all the booties, obtained in the battle of Hunain, among the*

---

1. Bukhari, p. 666, Hudud.
2. Muatta, p. 309, Ghalul.

Quraish and the tribes of Arabia excluding the Ansar,
they got angry and some murmured about it. So the
Holy Prophet called the Ansar and delivered an effective
oration to them in the month of Dhi'qa'dah, 8 A.H. at
Je'erranah:

عن ابي سعيد الخدري رضى الله عنه فاناهم رسول الله صلى الله
عليه وسلم فحمد الله و اثنى عليه ثم قال : يا معشر الانصار، ما قالة
بلغتنى عنكم ؟ وجدة وجدتموها على فى قلو بكم ؟ الم اجد كم ضلالا،
فهدا كم الله بى ؟ و كنتم اعداء متفرقين فالفكم الله بى ؟ و عالة فاغنا كم
الله بى، ؟ كلما قال شيأ، قالوا : الله و رسوله ابن و افضل ـ قال :
ما يمنعكم ان تجيبوا رسول الله معشر الا نصار ؟ قالو : بما ذا نجيبك
يا رسول الله ـ لله و لرسوله المن و الفضل ؟

"It is narrated from Abu Sa'id al-Khudri that the
Apostle of Allah, (peace be on him) came to them,
praised Allah, thanked Him and said: 'O tribe of Ansar,
what is the talk that has reached me from you? What
is this bitterness that you feel in your hearts against
me? Have I not found you going astray: and Allah
guided you through me? Disunited enemies; then Allah
united you through me? And needy; then Allah made you
rich through me?' Whenever he asked something, they
replied:' Allah and His Apostle are most bountiful and
graceful!' He said: 'What prevents you from replying to
the Apostle of Allah, O tribe of Ansar? They said: "What
should we reply, O Apostle of Allah, while all bounty and
grace belong to Allah and His Apostle'!"

ة

قال صلى الله عليه وسلم : اما و الله لو شئتم لقلتم فلصدقتم و لصدقتم : اتيتنا مكذبا فصدقناك، و مخذو لا فنصر ناك، و طريدا فآويناك، و عائلا فآسيناك -

He (may Allah send him peace and blessings!) said : "But, by Allah, if you like you may say--and you would be saying the truth and be justified: You came to us as disbelievers; but we believed in you; helpless, but we helped you; driven out, but we sheltered you; and a beggar, but we were munificent to you!"

اوجد تم على - يا معشرالانصار، - فى انفسكم فى لعاعة من الدليا تألفت بها قوما ليسلموا، ووكلتكم الى اسلامكم ؟ فانى اعطى رجالا حديثى عهد بكفر اتأ لفهم -

اما ترضون، يا معشرالانصار، ان يذهب الناس بالشاة و البعير و تذهبون برسول الله الى رحالكم ؟ فو الله لما تنقلبون به خير مما ينقلبون به -

لولا الهجرة لكنت من الا نصار - ولو سلك الناس و اديا و شعبا و سلكت الانصار واديا و شعبا لسلكت وادى الانصار و شعبها -

الانصار شعار و الناس دثار - انكم ستلقون بعدى اثرة شديدة فاصبروا حتى تلقوا الله و رسوله فانى على الحوض -

"Have you got angry with me, O tribe of Ansar for

a trifle worldly thing by which I court a people to stick to Islam while I rely upon your Islam? For I give some men, who were recently associated with infidelity, in order to mend their minds."

"Are you not pleased, O tribe of Ansar! that the people go with ewes and camels while you go along with the Apostle of Allah to your dwellings? By Allah, that with which you return is better than that with which they return."

"Had there been no Emigration I would have been one of the Ansar. If the people would go through a valley and passage, and the Ansar go through another valley and passage, and I would go through the valley and passage of the Ansar."

"The Ansar are the under-garment and the people are upper-garment. You will, surely, face after me a severe selfishness. Then have patience until you meet Allah and His Apostle. Verily I shall be on the Haud (pool water)."[1]

No. 16. *The oration was delivered by the Holy Prophet at Je'erranah in 8 A.H. about booties obtained in the battle of Hawazin when they embraced Islam and asked to return their properties and captives. He gave them option to take back either properties or captives. They accepted the latter.*

Then the Messenger of Allah--may Allah send him bliss and peace!--got up among the Muslims as

---

1. Bukhari, p. 620; Ibn Hisham with Zad, Vol. II, p. 305; Zad, Vol. II, p. 448.

speaker, praised Allah with what is due to Him and then he said:

اما بعد، فان اخوانكم قد جاؤ ونا تائبين و انا قد خيرنا هم بين
الذرارى و الاموال فلم يعدلوا بالا حساب شيأ ـ و انى قد رأيت ان ارد
اليهم سبيهم ـ

فمن احب منكم ان يطيب ذلك فليفعل ـ و من احب منكم ان
يكون على حظه فليعطنا و يكن قرضا علينا حتى نعطيه من اول ما
يفئى الله علينا، فليفعل ـ و اما من تمسك منكم بحقه من السبى،
فله بكل انسان ست قلائص ـ

فقال الناس: قد طيبنا ذلك يا رسول الله! فقال رسول الله صلى الله
عليه وسلم: انا لاندرى من اذن منكم فى ذلك ممن لم ياذن ـ
فارجعوا حتى يرفع الينا عرفاؤكم أمركم ـ

"As for the next, verily your brethren have come repentant and we have given them option between their offsprings and properties. But they have not considered anything equal to their pedigrees. I have decided to return their captives to them."

"So whosoever of you would like to be pleased with this, let him do it, and whosoever of you likes that he should retain his share he may give us and it may remain as a debt upon us, let him do it and we would repay it out of the first booty which Allah will bestow upon us. As regards him among you who retains his share of the captives, he will get six camels for one man."

"The peoples said: "O Apostle of Allah, we are willing to do that." The Apostle of Allah--peace and blessings of Allah be upon him--said: "Verily we do not know those of you who give consent to it and who do not. You, therefore, go back so that your chiefs will put forward to us your cases."[1]

No. 17 *The following invaluable oration was delivered by the Holy Prophet in Rajab, 9 A.H. at the field of Tabuk in Syria:*

فحمدالله و اثنى عليه بما هو اهله، ثم قال :

اما بعد، فان اصدق الحديث كتاب الله - و اوثق العرى كلمة التقوى -

وخير الملل ملة ابراهيم - وخير السنن سنة محمد -

و اشرف الحديث ذكر الله - و احسن القصص هذا القران -

وخير الامور عوازمها - و شر الامور محدثاتها - و احسن الهدى هدى الانبياء - و اشرف الموت قتل الشهداء -

واعمى العمى الضلالة بعد الهدى - وخير الاعمال مانفع - و خير الهدى ما اتبع و شر العمى عمى القلب - واليد العليا خير من اليد السفلى - ماقل و كفى خير مما كثر والنهى - وشر المعذرة حين يحضر الموت - وشر الندامة يوم القيامة -

So he praised Allah and thanked Him duly and said:

---

1. Bukhari, p. 618. Maghazi; Ibn Sa'd, Vol II, Pt I, p. 113. Battle of Hunain; Zaini, Vol. II. P. 131.

"Well, verily the most veracious discourse is the Book of Allah. The most trustworthy handhold is the word of piety.

"The best of the religions is the religion of Ibrahim. The best of the precedents is the precedents of Muhammad.

"The noblest speech is the invocation of Allah. The finest of the narratives is this Qur'an."

"The best of the affairs is that which has been firmly resolved upon. The worst things in religion are the newly created ones. The best of the ways is the way of the Prophets. The noblest death is the death of martyrs.

"The greatest blindness is going astray after guidance. The best of the actions is that which benefits. The best guidance is that which is followed (in practice). The worst blindness is the blindness of the heart. The upper hand is better than the lower hand. The little but sufficient is better than abundant but alluring. The worst apology is that which is made at the point of death. The worst regret is that which will be felt on the Day of Resurrection."

و من الناس من لايأتى الجمعة الا دبرا و منهم من لا يذكرالله الا هجرا-

و من اعظم الخطايا اللسان الكذاب و خير الغنى غنى النفس وخير الزاد التقوى ـ ورأس الحكمة مخافة الله عزوجل ـ وخير.ما و قرق القلوب اليقين ، والارتياب من الكفر ـ

والنياحة من عمل الجاهلية ـ والغلول من حر جهنم ـ والسكر
ى من النار ـ والشعر من ابليس ـ والخمر جماع الاثم ـ و شر المأكل
مال اليتيم ـ والسعيد من وعظ بغيره ـ والشقى من شقى فى بطن آمه ـ
وانما يدبر احد كم الى موضع اربعة اذرع ـ والامر الى الا خرة
و ملاك العمل خواتمه وشرالرؤيا رؤيا الكذب ـ و كل ما هو آت قريب ـ
سباب المؤمن فسوق و قتاله كفر ـ واكل لحمه من معصية الله و حرمة
ماله كحرمة دمه ـ

ومن يتألى على الله يكذبه ـ و من يغفر يغفر له ـ و من يعف يعف
الله عنه ـ

و من تكظم الغيظ يأجره الله ـ و من يصبر على الرزئية يعوضه الله
من يتبع السمعة يسمح الله به ـ ومن يتصبر يضا عف الله له ـ
و من يعص الله يعذبه الله ـ

واستغفر الله ـ و استغفر الله و استغفر الله ـ

"Some men do not come to Friday prayer but with delay. And some of them do not invocate Allah but with negligence.

"One of (the sources of) the greatest sins is the false tongue. The best richness is the richness of the soul. The best provision is piety. The highest philosophy is the fear of Allah, the Mighty and the Great. The best thing to be respected in the hearts is firm belief and the doubt is an infidelity.

"Waling is an act of ignorance. Betrayal is (the

cause of) the heat of Hell-fire. Drunkenness is (the cause of) causterisation by the Hell-fire. The (bad) poetry comes from devil. Wine is the centre of crimes. The worst food is the property of the orphan. Blessed is he who receives admonition from others. Wretched is he who becomes wretched in his mother's womb.

"Each one of you must resort to a place of four cubits (grave). (The issue of) the affair is (to be manifested) in the next life. The pivot of action is its ends. The worst dream is false dream. Whatever is to come is near. To abuse a believer is transgression and the fight against him is infidelity. To backbite him is a disobedience to Allah. Inviolability (and sacredness) of his property is like that of his blood (life).

"One who swears by Allah (falsely), He falsifies him. He who pardons (others), He pardons him. He who blots out (others' sins), Allah blots out his sins.

"He who represses the anger, Allah rewards him. He who perseveres in a misfortune, Allah indemnifies him.

"He who pursues renown (i.e. acts only for the sake of advertisement and being heard), Allah disgraces him. He who has patience, Allah gives him double. He who disobeys Allah, Allah chastises him.

" I beg pardon from Allah. I beg pardon from Allah. I beg pardon from Allah."[1]

---

1. Zad, Vol. II, p. 7

No. 18. *The following oration was delivered by the Holy Prophet when 'Adi ibn Hatim came first to the Prophet in 9 A.H.:*

عن عدى بن حاتم... فحمد الله و اثنى عليه ثم قال : ما يفرك؟
ايفرك ان تقول لا اله الا الله ؟ فهل تعلم من اله سوى الله ؟
قال : قلت لا ثم تكلم ساعة، ثم قال : اتفر ان يقال الله اكبر ـ
و هل تعلم شيأ اكبر من الله ؟ قال : قلت لا ـ قال : فان اليهود
مغضوب عليهم و ان النصارى ضالون ـ

It is reported from 'Adi ibn Hatim that the Apostle of Allah praised Allah and thanked Him; then said: "What puts you to flight? Does it put you to flight that you should say 'There is no god but Allah?' Do you know whether there is any god besides Allah?"

'Adi said: "I replied 'No'. Then the Holy Prophet spoke for a while, and then said: "You are, indeed, flying from the saying 'Allah is Great.' Do you know anything greater than Allah?" He said, I replied: 'No' (Then) he said: "Verily the Jews are the object of wrath (of Allah) and the Christians are astray."[1]

No. 19. *The following oration was delivered by the Holy Prophet after 'Adi ibn Hatim embraced Islam and a deputation of some hungry Madarites came to him at Madinah in 9 A.H.:*

---

1. Sad, Vol. I, p. 466

خطب فقال : ايها الناس! اتقوا ربكم الذى خلقكم من نفس
واحدة و خلق منها زوجها و بث منهما رجالا كثيرا ونساء ـ و اتقوا الله
الذى تساء لون به و الارحام ـ ان الله كان عليكم رقيبا ـ
و الاية التى فى الحشر: اتقوا الله و لتنظر نفس ما قدمت لغد ـ
يا ايها الناس، ارضحو امن الفضل ولو بصاع، ولو بنصف صاع،
ولو بقبضة، ولو ببعض قبضة ـ
يقى احد كم وجهه حر جهنم او النار، و لو بتدرة، ولو بشق تمرة
فان لم تجدوا فيكلمة طيبة ـ

He addressed thus: "O people, reverence your
Lord, Who created you from a single person: created
out of him, his mate and from them twain scattered
countless men and women;--reverence Allah, through
Whom you demand your mutual (rights), and
(reverence) the wombs that bore you; for Allah ever
watches over you. (Qur'an iv: 1)

"And he recited the verse which is in al-Hashr--
Fear Allah, and let everybody look to what (provision)
he sent forth in advance for the morrow.
(Qur'an xxxix: 18)

"O people, dole out from the surplus, though
it be one sa'(equivalent to three seers), though it be
half of a sa, though it be one handful and though
it be a part of one handful.

"Each one of you may save his face from the
heat of the Hell-fire though by means of one date and
though by means of apiece of date. If you do not have

(even such things then (save yourselves) by means of
a good word".

فان احد كم لاق الله و قائل له ما اقول لكم : الم اجعل لك
الا و ولدا؟ فيقول : بلى - فيقول اين ما قدمت لنفسك؟

فينظر قدامه له و بعده و عن يمينه و شماله ثم لا يجد شيئاً يقى به
وجهه حر جهنم -

ليتق احد كم وجهه النار و لو بشق تمرة، فان لم يجد فبكلما
طيبة -

فانى لا اخاف عليكم الفاقة - فان الله ناصر كم و معطيكم حتى
يسير الظعينة ما بين يثرب و الحيرة و أكثر ما يخاف على معطيته
السرق -

. . . . و قال : من سن فى الاسلام سنة حسنة فله اجرها و اجر من
عمل بها من بعده من غير ان ينقص من اجورهم شيئى - و من سن فى
الاسلام سنة سيئة كان عليه و زرها و وزر من عمل بها من بعده من
غير ان ينقص من اوزار هم شيئى -

"Surely each one of you will meet Allah and
He will ask him what I am saying: 'Did I not give
you wealth and children?' He will reply: 'Yes', Then
Allah will say: 'Where is that which you have sent
in advance for your soul?'

"So he will look to his front and behind; to the
right and the left. But he will not find anything to
save his face from the heat of the Hell-fire.

"Each one of you should save his face from
the Fire though by means of a piece of date. If he

has nothing (to offer), then (do it even) by means of a good word.

"For I do not fear hunger for you. Because Allah will help you and give you plenty so much so that woman on a litter will travel from Yathrib (Madinah) to Hirah (alone), or more, while there will be no fear of theft on her riding beast.

"...And (then) he said: "Whosoever introduces a good usage in Islam, there is for him its reward along with the (equivalent) reward of those who act up it after him without anything being diminished from their rewards. And whosoever introduces a bad usage in Islam, there is upon him its sin and (equivalent) sin of those who act up it after him without anything being diminished from their sins,"[1]

No. 20. *The following oration was delivered by the Holy Prophet in 9 A.H. when the deputation of Banu-Muntafiq came to him:*

قال لقيط بن عامر رضى الله عنه : قد منا على رسول الله صلى الله عليه و سلم ـ فوا فيناه حين انصرف من صلوة الغداة فقام فى الناس خطيبا فقال :

ايها الناس، الاآن قد خبأت لكم صوتى منذ اربعة ايام الا لتسمعوا اليوم ـ الا فهل من امرئ بعثه قومه فقالوا له ٠ اعلم لنا مأ يقول رسول الله صلى الله عليه و سلم ـ الاثم رجل لعله يلهيه حديث نفسه او حديث

---

1. Muslim with Nawawi, (Delhi, ed) Vol. I. p. 327, Zakat; Zad, Vol. I. p. 466, deputation

صاحبه او يلهيه ضال الا انى مسئول هل بلغت ـ الا اسمعوا تعيشوا ـ
الا اجلسوا فجلس الناس ـ

قلت يا رسول الله ! ما عندك من علم الغيب ؟ فضحك فقال : لعمر
الله، اعلم انى ابتغى السقطة فقال : ضن ربك بمفاتيح خمس من الغيب ـ
لا يعلمها الا الله :

علم المنية قد علم متى منية احدكم ولا تعلمونه و علم المنى
حين يكون فى الرحم، قد علمه و لا تعلمونه و علم ما فى غد، قد علم
ما الت طاعم ولا تعلمه و علم يوم الغيث، يشرف عليكم ازلين مشفقين
فيظل يضحك، قد علم ان غوثكم الى قريب و علم الساعة،

ثم تلبثون ما لبثتم تبعث الصائحة ـ فلعمر الهك ما تدع على ظهر
ها شيأ الا مات تلبثون ما لبثتم ـ ثم يتوفى نبيكم و الملائكة الذين مع
ربك ـ

فاصبح ربك عز و جل يطوف فى الارض و خلت عليه البلاد :
فارسل ربك السماء تهضب من عند العرش ـ

فلعمر الهك ما تدع على ظهر ها من مصرع قتيل ولا مدفن ميت
الا شقت القبر عنه حتى تخلفه من عند رأسه فيستوى حالسا ـ فيقول
ربك : مهيم ؟ لما كان فيه ـ يقول : يا رب، امس اليوم لعهده بالحياة
يحسبه حديثا باهه ـ

Laqit ibn 'Amir said: "We came to the Apostle
of Allah (may Allah send him peace and bliss!) and
we saw him when he was off from the morning prayer.
Then he stood up among the people as a speaker
and said:

"O people, behold, I have withheld my voice
among you for four days, so that you shall listen to

it today. Lo, is there anybody whom his people have
sent and asked him: 'Learn for us what the Apostle
of Allah (may Allah send him peace and bliss!) says?'
Then the man, perhaps diverted by his own affair or
the affair of his companion, or is diverted by someone
going astray. Beware, I shall be asked whether I have
conveyed (the Message of Allah). Lo, harken so that
you may live. Please, take your seats. So people took
their seats."

I said: "O Apostle of Allah, what knowledge of
unseen have you got?" He laughed and replied: "By
the name (or religion) of Allah, know that I am to
seek the fallen things." Then he added: "Allah has
not given the key of five unseen things to anyone.
None knows them except Allah.

"(Among them is) the knowledge of death; verily
He knows when each one of you will die and you
do not know it. The knowledge of semen when it
goes into the womb. He knows it and you do not
know it. The knowledge of what will be tomorrow;
verily He knows what you will eat (tomorrow), and
you do not know it. The knowledge of the day of
raining; He looks at you while you are afflicted with
severities and you are disappointed. Then He begins
to laugh; because He knows that it will rain soon.
And (the last is) the knowledge of resurrection.

"Hereafter you will stay (in this world) as long
as you are to stay. Then the trumpet will be blown.
By the name of Allah, it will leave nothing upon the
surface of the earth but dead. You will stay as long

as you are to stay. Then your Prophet and the angels--
who are with your Lord--will be dead.

"Then your Lord (the Mighty and Glorious) will
go round the earth; and countries will be empty. Then
your Lord will send the heavy rain from near the
Throne.

"By the name of your Allah, it will leave upon
the surface of it, neither a fighting-place of a killed
one nor a burial-ground of a dead body, but will split
his grave asunder and it will repair him beginning from
his head. Then he will sit aright. Then your Lord will
say: What is the matter? meaning how long he stayed
there. He will reply: O my lord, only yesterday, because
of his connection with this life, he will think that he
had been recently connected with his family."

فقلت : يا رسول الله فكيف يجمعنا بعد ما تمزقنا الرياح و البلاء
و السباع ؟

قال : انبئك بمثل ذلك فى الاء الله : الارض اشرفت عليها و هى
مدرة بالية ـ فقلت لا تحيى ابدا ـ ثم ارسل الله عليك السماء، فلم تلبث
عليها الا ايا ما حتى اشرفت عليها و هى شربة واحدة ـ

و لعمر الهك لهو اقدر على ان يجمعكم من الماء على ان يجمع
نبات الارض ـ تتخر جون من الاصواء و من مصار عكم فتنتظرون اليه
و ينظر اليكم ـ

قلت : يا رسول الله ! كيف و نحن ملا الارض و هو شخص واحد
ينظر الينا و ننظر اليه ؟

قال انبئك بمثل هذا فى آلاء الله : الشمس و القمر آية منه صغيرة۔ ترونهما و تريانكم ساعة واحدة ولا تضامون فى رويتهما ۔

قلت يا رسول الله، فما يفعل بنا ربنا اذا لقيناه ؟

قال : تعرضون عليه بادية له صفحانكم لا يخفى عليه منكم خافية۔ فيأخذ ربك عز و جل بيده عرفة من ماء فينضح بها قبلكم - فلعمر الهك ما يخطى وجه احد منكم منها قطرة ۔

فاما المسلم فتدع وجهه مثل الريطة البيضاء و اما الكافر فينضحه بمثل الحمم الاسود ۔

الاثم ينصرف نبيكم و نفرق على اثره الصالحون فيسلكون جسرا من النار، يطأ احد۔ كم الجمرة يقول حس - يقول ربك عز و جل : اوانه ۔

الا فتطلعون على حوض نبيكم على اظماء ۔ والله ۔ ناهلة قط ما رايتها ۔

فلعمر الهك ما يبسط احد منكم يده الا وقع عليها قدح بطهره من الطوف و البول و الاذى ۔

و تحتبس الشمس و القمر - فلا ترون منهما واحدا ۔

I said: "O Apostle of Allah, how will He gather us after our being scattered by the winds, consumptions and beasts."

He said: " I shall explain it to you drawing an example from the (created) favours of Allah (natural phenomena) : you have come across a land while it is dry and waste. So you have said that it would never be fertile. Then Allah has sent down rain upon you. After only a few days you have visited while it is full of green.

"By the name of Allah, He is, indeed, more powerful over gathering (reviving) you than the water to return the green of the earth to life. Thus you will be brought forth from your graves and the places where you were thrown. Then you will look at Him and He will look at you.

I said: "O Apostle of Allah, we are worldful and He is only one; how will He look at us and will we look at Him (at a time)?"

He said: "I will show you the like of it in the favours of Allah (phenomena): The sun and the moon are a little sign of Him. You see both of them and they see you at a time without clash for their sight".

I asked: "O Apostle of Allah, what will our Lord do with us when we meet Him?"

He replied: "You will be exposed to Him and all your sides will be manifest to Him. Nothing of you will remain concealed from Him. Then your Lord, (the Mighty and Exalted), will take up a handful of water and sprinkle it on you. By the name of your Lord, no face of yours will miss a drop of it.

'As a result, it will leave the face of the Muslim like a white sheet; but as regards the infidel it will burn him thoroughly like black charcoals.

"Behold, then your Prophet will depart and the good ones will follow him. Then they will come across a bridge of fire; every one of you stepping on the charcoal and saying 'Oh!' Your Lord, (the Mighty and Great), will say: 'Yes' (now is the proper time).

"Lo, then you will come on the 'Haud' (pool of water) of your Prophet with an extreme thirst for a draught of water which, by Allah, I have never seen.

"By the name of Allah, none of you will stretch out his hand but a cup of water will come down to him which will purify him from ordure, urine, and other unclean things."

"And the sun and the moon will be concealed such as you will not see either of the two."

قلت : يا رسول الله ! فبم نبصر ؟ قال : بمثل بصرك ساعتك هذه، و ذاك مع طلوع الشمس فى يوم اشرقت الارض و واجهت به ألجبال ـ

قلت : يا رسول الله ! فبم تجزئ من سيئاتنا و حسناتنا ؟

قال : الحسنة بعشر امثالها والسيئة بمثلها الا ان يعفو ـ

قلت : يا رسول الله ! ما الجنة و ما النار ؟

قال : لعمر الهك ان النار لها سبعة ابواب ما منها بابان الا يسير الراكب بينهما سبعين عاما ـ و ان الجنة لها ثمانية ابواب ما منها بابان الا يسير الراكب بينهما سبعين عاما ـ

قلت : يا رسول الله ! فعلى ما نطلع من الجنة ؟

I said: "O Apostle of Allah, then how shall we see?" He replied: (You will see) as you see just now. It is as you do with the sunrise on a particular day when the earth is shining and the hills have come in between."

I enquired: " O Apostle of Allah, how will our evil

and good deeds be requited?"

He replied: "The good deeds (will be requited) ten times and the bad deeds one time, save He forgives."

I inquired: " O Apostle of Allah, what are the Heaven and the Hell?"

He answered: "By the name of your Allah, verily the Hell has got seven gates; there are no two gates but a horseman can travel between them for seventy years. And the Heaven has got eight gates; between any two gates the horseman can travel for seventy years."

I asked: "O Apostle of Allah, upon which part of the Heaven shall we appear?"

قال : على انهار من عسل مصفى ، و انهار من حمر ماء بها صداع و ندامة، و انهار من لبن ما يتغير طعمه ، وماء غير اسن ، و فاكهة ، ولعمر الهك ـ ما تعلمون و خير من مثله معه ازواج مطهرة ـ

قلت : يا رسول الله ! اولنا فيها ازواج و منهن مصلحات ؟

قال : المصلحات للصالحين ـ و فى لفظ : الصالحات للصالحين تلذ و نهن و يلذونكم [1] مثل لذاتكم فى الدنيا غير ان لا توالد ـ

قلت : يا رسول الله ! علام ابا يعك ؟ فبسط النبى (صلى الله عليه وسلم) يده و قال : على اقام الصلوة و ايتاء الزكوة و زيال المشرك، و ان لا تشرك بالله انها غيره ـ

قلت : يا رسول الله ! و ان لنا مابين المشرق و المغرب نحل منها حيث شئنا ولا يجنى على امرى' الا نفسه ؟

قال : ذلك ' تحل حيث شئت و لا يجنى عليك الا نفسك ـ

1. كذاق الا صل

He replied : "Upon rivers of pure honey, streams
of wine having in it no headache and regret; streams
of milk, the taste of which will not be altered; of water
which is not stagnant; and upon fruits; and by the name
of your Lord, upon something better than this which you
do not know; in addition there will be many clean wives."

I said: "O Apostle of Allah, would there be wives
and some of them very good?"

He said : "The good ones will get good wives. And
according to another version--the virtuous women are for
virtuous ones. You will delight in them and they will
delight in you like your delights in this world except that
there will be no begetting."

I asked: "O Apostle of Allah, on what shall we take
our oath of allegiance to you." So he stretched his hand
and said: "On the performance of prayer, giving poor-
rates, dissociation from the polytheists, and that you will
not make any god a partner of Allah."

I inquired: "O Apostle of Allah, and shall we have
(then) whatever is between the east and the west, so
that we can alight wherever we like and no one will
commit an offence except himself on his behalf?"

He said:" That is right; you may alight wherever

you like and except yourself none will commit an offence on your behalf."

قال : فالنصر فنا عنه ـ ثم قان : ها ان ذين ، ها ان ذين ، مرتين ـ من اتقى الناس فى الا ولى والآخرة ـ

فقال : كعب بن الجذارية : من هم يا رسول الله ؟

قال : بنوا المنتفق ـ بنوا المنتفق، بنوا المنتفق اهل ذلك منهم ـ

قال : فانصر فنا و اقبلت عليه فقلت : يا رسول الله ! هل لا حه ممن مضى من خير جاهليتهم ؟

فقال رجل من عرض قريش : والله ان اباك المنتفق لفى النار ـ

فقلت : يا رسول الله ! و اهلك ؟

قال : و اهلى لعمر الله ـ حيث ما اتيت على قبر عامرى او قرشى او دوسى، قل ارسلنى اليك محد (صلى الله عليه وسلم) فا بشر بما يسوكك تجر على و جهك و بطنك فى النار ـ

قلت : يا رسول الله ! و ما فعل بهم ذلك ؟ و قد كانوا على عمل لا يحسنون الا اياه، و كانوا يحسبون انهم مصلحون ـ

قال : ذلك بان الله بعث فى اخر كل سبع امم نبيا ـ فمن عصى تبيه كان من الضالين ـ و من اطاع نبيه كان من المهتدين ـ

Laqit said: "We departed from him. Then he said: 'Lo these two--lo--, these two--twice--belong to the most pious class of people in this world and the next."

Then Ka'b ibn al Jedhariyah asked: 'Who are they, O Apostle of Allah?

He replied: "(They are) Banu'l-Muntafiq, Banu'l-Muntafiq, Banu'l-Muntafiq. Among them are those who deserve this."

Laqit said: 'Then we returned again to his front and I asked: "O Apostle of Allah, will anyone, from among those who have passed away in the pagan age, have any good?"

In the meantime, an ordinary man of the Quraishites said: "By Allah verily your father Muntafiq is, indeed, in the Hell."

So I said: "O Apostle of Allah, what about of your ancestors?"

He said: "My ancestors fare the same, by Allah. Wherever you come across the grave of a man belonging to the tribe of 'Amer of Quraish or Daus, say, Muhammad--(may Allah send His blessings and peace to him)--sent me (to say) so rejoice at your misfortunes. You will be dragged down on your face and belly in the Fire."

I said: "O Apostle of Allah, why will they be treated so while they did only whatever they considered good and thought that they were right?"

He replied: "It is because Allah sent a Prophet to the last of every seven nations. So he who disobeyed his Prophet, is from among those going astray; and he, who obeyed his Prophet, is from among those going aright."[1]

No. 21. *The following oration was delivered by the Holy Prophet most probably in 9 or 10 A.H. after the Hajj was made obligatory (vide* Sirat-un-Nabi, Shibli).

عن ابی هریره رضی الله عنه خطب رسول الله صلی الله علیه وسلم الناس،
فقال : یا ایها الناس ! ان الله عز و جل قد فرض علیکم الحج فحجوا -
فقال رجل (اقرع بن حابس) افی کل عام یا رسول الله ؟ فسکت عنه
حتی اعاده ثلثا فقال : لو قلت نعم لو جبت - ولو وجبت ما اقمتم بها -
ذرونی ما ترکتکم - فانما هلک من کان قبلکم بکثرة سوالهم و اختلافهم
علی انبیائهم - فاذا امرتکم بشئی فخذوا منه ما استطعتم - و اذا نهیتکم
عن شئی فاجتنبوه

It is reported by Abu Hurairah that the Apostle of Allah--may Allah grant him peace and blessing!- delivered a speech to the people. So he said: "O People, verily Allah, the Mighty and Great, has made the pilgrimage incumbent on you. So make pilgrimage." In the meanwhile a man (Aqru' ibn Habis) inquired: O Apostle of Allah, whether every year?" He said remained silent till the man repeated the question thrice. So he said: "If I say 'yes' it will surely become obligatory and if it becomes obligatory you will not

---

1. Zad, Vol. II, p. 51 with an authentic chain of narrations.

execute it. Let me alone as long as I do so. Your fore-
runners perished, indeed, on account of their multiplicity
of questions and their diversification from their prophets.
So when I bid you anything, do it as far as you can;
and when I forbid .you anything, avoid it."[1]

No. 22. *The following oration was delivered by the
Holy Prophet in 9. A.H. (vide Shibli, Sirat-un-Nabi, Vol.II,
pp. 71, 72).*

فحمد الله و اثنى عليه ثم قال : اما بعد ، فانى استعمل الرجل منكم
على العمل مما و لانى الله فياتى فيقول : هذا لكم و هذا هدية اهديت لى ـ
افلا جلس فى بيت ابيه و امه فينظر ايهدى له ام لا ان كان صادقا ؟
والذى نفس محمد بيده ، لا ياخذ احد منكم شيئاً بغير حقه الا لقى الله يحمله
يوم القيامة ـ

He praised Allah and thanked Him; then he said:
"As for next, verily I appoint an officer from among
you for which Allah gave me authority. Then he returns
and says, 'this is for you and this is a present
presented to me." Why then does he not sit down
in the house of his father and mother and then see
whether presents are given to him or not if he is
true? By Him in whose hand is the life of Muhammad,
nobody will take anything without right, he will meet
Allah carrying it on the Day of Resurrection.

---

1. Mishkat : Hajj ; Tirmidhi : Hajj ; Muslim : Hajj.

لا الفين احدكم يجئى يوم القيامة على رقبته بغير له رغاء يقول : يا
رسول الله ! يجئى اغثنى ـ فاقول : لا املك لك شيئاً قد ابلغتك ـ

لا الفين احدكم يجئى يوم القيامة على رقبته فرس له حمحمة، فيقول:
يا رسول الله اغثنى ـ فأقول : لا املك لك شيأ قد ابلغتك ـ

لا الفين احد كم يجئى يوم القيامة على رقبة شاة لها ثغاء، يقول :
يا رسول الله اغثنى فاقول : لا املك لك شيأ، قد ابلغتك

لأ الفين احدكم يجئى يوم القيامة على رقبته لفس لها صياح، فيقول:
يا رسول الله ! اغثنى ـ فاقول : لا املك لك شيأ، قد ابلغتك

لا الفين احد كم يجئى يوم القيامة على رقبته رقاع تخفق، فيقول: يا
رسول الله ! اغثنى ـ فاقول : لا املك لك شيأ ـ قد ابلغتك ـ

لا الفين احد كم يجئى يوم القيامة على رقبته صامت، فيقول : يا
رسول الله ! اغثنى ـ فاقول: لا املك لك شيأ قد ابلغتك ـ

ثم رفع يديه حتى رأينا عفرة ابطيه ـ ثم قال : اللهم هل بلغت ؟
اللهم هل بلغت ؟ بصر عينى وسمع اذنى ـ

"I should never find anyone of you--coming on the
Day of Resurrection with a grumbling camel on his neck--
saying 'O Apostle of Allah, help me!' But I shall then say,
'I cannot help you in the least; I have already conveyed
you the message.'

I should never find anyone of you--coming on
the Day of Resurrection with a neighing horse on his
neck,--saying 'O Apostle of Allah, help me.' But I shall

say, 'I cannot help you in the least; I have already conveyed you the message.'

I should never find any one of you--coming on the day of Resurrection with a bleating goat on his neck,-- saying 'O Apostle of Allah, help me.' But I shall say, I cannot help you in the least; I have already conveyed you the message.'

I should never find anyone of you--coming on the Day of Resurrection with a crying soul on his neck,-- saying 'O Apostle of Allah, help me.' But I shall say, ' I cannot help you in the least; I have already conveyed you the message.'

I should never find anyone of you--coming on the Day of Resurrection with fluttering patches on his neck,-- saying 'O Apostle of Allah, help me'. I shall then reply, I cannot help you in the least; I have already conveyed you the message.'

I should never find anyone of you--coming on the Day of Resurrection with some mute property on his neck,--saying 'O Apostle of Allah, help me.' I shall then say I cannot help you in the least; I have (already) conveyed you the message."

Then the Apostle of Allah raised his hands so much that we saw the whiteness of his two armpits. Then he said: "O Allah, have I communicated? O Allah! Have I communicated? I am an eye and ear-witness of it."[1]

---

1. Muslim with Nawawi (ed. Delhi). Vol. II pp. 122, 123; Bukhari, p. 353, 432, 1033, 1064, 1068; Abu Da'ud, Hadaya'-l 'Ummal.

No. 23. *The following oration was delivered by the Holy Prophet in the beginning of 10 A.H., when Ibrahim, a son of the Prophet, died and on the same day the sun eclipsed. So people said that the sun eclipsed for the death of Ibrahim.*

فخطب خطبة بليغة ، فحمد الله و اثنى عليه ـ و شهد ان لا اله الا الله، و انه عبده و رسوله ـ ثم قال ـ

ايها الناس ! انشد كم بالله ـ هل تعلمون انى قصرت فى شيئى من تبليغ رسالات ربى ؟ لما اخبر تمونى بذلك ـ

So he delivered an eloquent speech to the people. He praised Allah, thanked Him, bore witness that there is no god but Allah and he is His bond and His Apostle. Then he said:

"O people I adjure you, by Allah, do you know whether I have fallen short in the delivery of my Lord's message?--you must inform me of that."

قال رجل : نشهد انك قد بلغت رسالات ربك، و نصحت لا متك و قضيت الذى عليك ـ

A man said: "We bear witness that you have conveyed the messages of your Lord, advised your people and done your duty."

ثم قال : اما بعد، ان ناسا بزعمون ان الشمس والقمر لا ينكسفان الا لموت عظيم من العظماء، و ليس كذلك، و انهم قد كذبوا - ان الشمس و القمر ايتان من ايات الله - لا يخسفان لموت احد ولا لحياته، - ولكنهما خليقتان من خلقه - يحدث الله فى خلقه ما يشاء - و يخوف الله بهما عباده، و يعتبر بهما عباده، فينظر من يحدث منه توبه -

فاذا رأيتم شيأ من ذلك، فادعوا الله و كبروا وافزعوا الى الصلوة و تصدقوا واذكروا الله كثيرا - حتى ينجلى او يحدث الله امرا -

يا امة محمد! والله ما احد اغير من الله ان يزنى عبده او تزنى امته -

يا امة محمد! لو تعلمون ما اعلم لضحكتم قليلا و لبكيتم كثيرا -

و ايم الله، لقد رأيت منذ قمت اصلى ما انتم لا قوه من امر ديناكم و اخرتكم -

وانه - والله - لا تقوم الساعة حتى يخرج ثلثون كذابا - و اخرهم الاعور الدجال ممسوح العين اليسرى كأنها عين ابى يحيى - شيخ حينئذ من الانصار بينه و بين حجرة عائشة رضى الله عنها وانه متى يخرج فسوف يزعم انه الله فمن - امن به و صدقه واتبعه لم ينفعه صالح من عمله سلف - و من كفربه و كذبه لم يعاقب بشيئى من عمله سلف -

وانه سيظهر على الارض كلها الا على الحرم و بيت المقدس - وانه محصر المؤمنين فى بيت المقدس - فيتزلزلونزلزالا شديدا -

Then he said: "Now to proceed, verily people assume that the sun and the moon do not eclipse but for the death of a great man. It is not so and they are wrong in their opinions. Verily the sun and the moon are two signs of Allah. They do not eclipse for the death and life of anyone. But they are two created things from among His creation. Allah creates in His creation whatever He likes. Allah warns His bonds through them and makes (the bonds) to get a lesson from them, then He sees who from among them repents."

"So when you see such a thing, call Allah, say Takbir, hasten to the prayer, give alms and frequent the remembrance of Allah till it clears off or Allah creates a (new) thing."

"O people of Muhammad, by Allah, there is none more jealous (intolerant) than Allah of His servant who commits adultery or His woman servant who does the same."

"O people of Muhammad, by Allah, if you know what I know would surely laugh little and weep much."

"By Allah, since I have been standing in my prayer, I have seen what you have to come across the affair of this world and the next."

"By Allah, the Hour will not come until and unless thirty liars appear. The last of them is the one eyed Dajjal (Deceiver) whose left eye is rubbed off as if it is the eye of Abu Yahya--an old man of the Ansar who was then between him and the chamber of Ai'sha. And verily when he will appear, soon he will say that he is God. So he who believes in him, (then) no previous good action will give him any benefit. And he who disobeys him, he will not be retailed for any of his previous (bad) actions."

"Verily he will soon overcome the whole world except the Haram (the sacred sanctuary of Mecca and Madinah) and Jerusalem. He will besiege the believers in Jerusalem. So that they will be shaken a great shaking."

ثم يهلكه الله عزو جل و جنوده حتى ان حرم الحائط ـ او قال: اصل الحائط او اصل الشجرة ـ لينادى يا مسلم! يا مومن! هذا يهودى ـ او قال كافر ـ فتعال فاقتله ـ

و لن يكون ذلك حتى تروا امورا يتفاقم بينكم شانها فاق انفسكم و تسائلون بينكم هل كان نبيكم ذكر لكم منها ذكرا ـ و حتى تزول جبال عن مراتبها ـ ثم على اثر ذلك القبض ـ

و لقد أوحى الى انكم تفتنون فى القبور مثل او قريبا من ـ فتنة المسيح الدجال يوفى احد كم فيقال له : ما علمك بهذا الرجل؟

فاما المؤمن ـ او قال المؤمن : فيقول : محد رسول الله ، جائنا بالبينات والهدى، قاجبنا و امنا واتبعنا و صدقنا ـ فيقال له : نم صالحا ـ قد كنا نعلم ان كنت لمؤمنا به ـ

و اما المنافق ـ او المرتاب ـ فيقال له : ما علمك بهذا الرجل؟ فيقول : لا ادرى، سمعت الناس يقولون شيأ فقلته ـ

"Then Allah,--the Mighty and Exalted,--will destroy him and his armies, even the sanctuary of the wall--or he said, foot of the wall--or root of the tree will cry; O Muslim! O Mumin! here is a Jew--or he said,--here is an infidel; come and kill him!'

"And it will not take place until you see affairs which will ask one another whether your Prophet has mentioned anything concerning them, and until the mountains will be displaced from their stations. After that is the Resurrection.

"It is, indeed, revealed to me that you will be put to test in the graves like the very test with the Anti-Christ. Each one of you will be approached and asked, 'What do you know of this man?'

"As regards the believer, he will say: 'He is Muhammad, the Apostle of Allah, who came to us with clear evidences and guidance. So we responded, believed, followed and accepted (him) as true' So it will be said to him, 'Have a sound sleep. We are aware that you were, indeed, a believer in him'

"As regards the hypocrite--or he said,'wavering'--it will be said to him 'What do you know about this man ?' He will say, ' I do not know; I heard the people saying something; so I said so'."

قالو ! يا رسول الله ! رأيناك تناولت شيئاً فى مقامك هذا، ثم رأيناك تكعكعت !

فقال انى رأيت الجنة، فتناولت منها عنقودا حين رأيتمونى اتقدم ـ لو اخذته لا كلتم منه ما بقيت الدنيا ـ

و رأيت النار يحطم بعضها بعضا حين رأيتمونى تاخرت ـ فلم ار كاليوم منظرا قط افظع منها حتى لقد جعلت اتقيها خشية ان تغشا كم ـ

حتى رأيت فيها امرأة من حمير تعذب فى هرة ربطتها، فلم تدعها
تأكل من حشاش الارض ـ فلاهى اطعمتها و لا هى سقتها حتى ماتت ـ
فلقد رأيتها تنهشها اذا اقبلت ، و اذا ولت تنهش اليتها ـ

و حتى رأيت فيها صاحب السبتيتين اخا بنى الدعدع يدفع بعضا
ذات شعبتين فى النار ـ

و حتى رأيت فيها صاحب المحجن الذى كان يسرق الحاج بمحجنه
متكئا على محجنه فى النار يقول : انا سارق المحجن ـ

و رأيت أكثر اهل النار النساء ـ قالوا : بم يا رسول الله ؟ قال :
بكفرهن ـ قيل : ايكفرن بالله ؟ قال : يكفرن العشير و يكفرن الاحسان ـ
و لو احسنت الى احداهن الدهر كله ، ثم رأت منك شيأ ، قالت : ما رأيت
منك خيرا قط ـ

They said, "O Apostle of Allah, we have seen you
catching something in this stand; after a while we have
seen you stepping back!"

He said: Verily I have seen the Heaven; and
caught a bunch of grapes from it when you have
seen me going forward. Had I taken it you would
eat it as long as the world would last."

"And I have seen the Hell-fire breaking each
other when you have seen me stepping back. I have
never seen a scene more dreadful as I did today
so much that I began to guard against it fearing that
it may envelop you."

"I have seen in it a woman of Himyar being
punished for a she-cat which she tied (in her life

time) and did not let loose to eat any residue on the earth. Neither she fed it, nor gave it anything to drink, and as a result, it died. So I have seen it biting her when she came forward and biting her buttocks when she retreated.

"I have seen there a man, with a pair of leather-shoes, brother of Banu Da'da', pushing someone having two twigs of a tree into the Fire.

"I have seen there a man, with a hooked stick who used to steal the pilgrims with it, leaning upon it in the Hell saying, 'I used to steal with the hook.'

"I have seen that the majority of the people of the Hell was the women. They asked: Why, O Apostle of Allah? He said: On account of their un-gratefulness. Someone said: Are they ungrateful to Allah? He replied: They are ungrateful to their relation (husband) and they are ungrateful to good (done to them). If you do good to any of them all the while, then she sees anything (unpleasant) from you, she says: 'I never saw any good from you.'"[1]

No. 24--*The following memorable oration was delivered by the Holy Prophet during his Farewell Pilgrimage in Batnu'l-Wadi of 'Arafat on Thursday, 9th Dhu'l-Hijjah, 10 A.H.*

الحمد لله ـ نحمده و نستعينه و نستغفره و نتوب اليه ـ و نعوذ بالله من شرور انفسنا و من سيئات اعمالنا ـ من يهد الله فلا مضل له ـ ومن

---

1. Bukhari, pp. 18, 142, 143, 144, 145; Nasa'i (ed. Delhi, Ansari Press), Vol. 1 pp. 151, 152, 153, 154; Mishkat, Kusuf ; Zad Vol. I p. 127.

يضلل فلا هادى له ـ و اشهد ان لا اله الا الله وحده لا شريك له ـ و
اشهد ان محمداً عبده و رسوله ـ اوصيكم عباد الله ! بتقوى الله و احثكم
على طاعته واستفتح بالذى هو خير ـ

"All praise is for Allah, We praise Him; seek His
help and pardon; and we turn to Him. We take refuge
with Allah from the evils of ourselves and from the bad
consequences of our actions. There is none to led him
astray whom Allah guides aright and there is none to
guide him aright whom He misguides. I bear witness that
there is no god but Allah alone without any partner, I
bear witness that Muhammad is His bond and His
Apostle. I admonish you, O bonds of Allah, to fear Allah
and I urge you on His obedience and I open the speech
with that which is good."

اما بعد، ايها الناس ! اسمعوا منى، ابين لكم ـ فانى لا ادرى، لعلى
لا القاكم بعد عامى هذا فى موقفى هذا ابدا ـ
ايها الناس ! ان دماءكم و اموالكم و اعراضكم عليكم حرام الى ان
تلقوا ربكم كحرمة يومكم هذا، فى شهركم هذا، فى بلدكم هذا ـ وانكم
ستلقون ربكم فيسئلكم من اعمالكم ـ الا هل بلغت ؟ اللهم فاشهد ـ
فمن كانت عنده امانة فليودها الى من ائتمنه عليها ـ
الا لا يجنى جان الا على نفسه ـ الا لا يجنى جان على ولده، ولا
مولود على والده ـ

"Now to proceed, O people, listen to me; I would
deliver a message to you. For I do not know whether
I shall ever get an opportunity to meet you after this year
in this place.

"O people, verily your blood (lives), your properties and your honour are sacred and inviolable to you till you appear before your Lord, like the sacredness of this day of yours, in this month of yours, in this city of yours. Verily you will meet your Lord and He will ask you about your actions. Lo, Have I conveyed the message? O Allah, be witness."

"So he who has any trust with him he should restore it to the person who deposited it with him.

"Be aware, no one committing a crime is responsible for it but himself. Neither son is responsible for the crime of his father nor father is responsible for the crime of his son."

نفسه ـ فلا تظلمن انفسكم ـ اللهم هل بلغت ؟

الا كل شيئى من امر الجاهلية تحت قدمى موضوع ـ دماء الجاهلية موضوعة ـ و ان اول دم اضع من دمائنا دم ابن ربيعة بن الحارث ـ و كان مستر ضعا فى بنى سعد، فقتلته هذيل ـ

و ربا الجاهلية موضوع ـ ولكن لكم رؤوس اموالكم ـ لا تظلمون ولا تظلمون ـ قضى الله انه لا ربا ـ و اول ربا اضع من ربائنا ربا عباس بن عبد المطلب ـ فاله موضوع كله ـ

ايها الناس ! فاتقوا الله فى النساء ـ فانكم اخذ تموهن بامانة الله ـ و استحلم فروجهن يكلمة الله ـ

ان لكم على نسائكم حقا ، ـ و لنسائكم عليكم حقا ـ لكم عليهن ان
لا يوطئن فرشكم احدا تكرهون ـ ولا ياذن فى بيوتكم لمن تكرهون ـ فان
فعلن ذلك فان الله اذن لكم ان تعضلوهن و تهجر و هن فى المضاجع و
تضربوهن ضربا غير مبرح ـ فان انتهين فلهن عليكم رزقهن و كسوتهن
بالمعروف ـ

"Lo O people, listen to my words and understand
them. You must know that the Muslim is the brother of
the Muslim and the Muslims are one brotherhood.
Nothing of his brother is lawful for a Muslim except
what he himself allows. So you should not oppress
yourselves. O Allah, have I conveyed the message?

'Behold, everything of Ignorance is put down
under my two feet. The blood-revenges of the Dark
Age are remitted. Verily, the first blood-revenge I
cancel is the blood-revenge of Ibn Rabi'ah ibn Harith
who was nursed in the tribe of Sa'd and whom the
Hudhail killed.

"The interest of the *jahiliyyah* period is abolished.
But you will get your capital-stock. Do not oppress and
you will not be oppressed. Allah has decreed that there
is no interest. The first interest which I cancel is that of
'Abbas ibn 'Abdul-Muttalib. Verily it is cancelled entirely.

"O people, do fear Allah concerning the women.
You have taken with the trust of Allah and you have
made their private parts lawful with word of Allah.

"Verily you have got certain right over your
women and your women have certain right over you.
Your right over them is that they should not make

anybody, whom you dislike, trample down your beds, and that they should not allow any one whom you dislike (to enter) into your houses. If they do such an action, then Allah permitted you to harass them. keep them separate in their beds and beat them but not soverely. If they refrain, they must have justly their sustenance and clothing from you."

الا واستوصوا بالنساء خيرا ـ فانهن عوان عندكم ـ لا يملكن لا نفسهن شيأ ـ وليس تملكون منهن شيأ غير ذلك ـ فان اطعنكم فلا تبغوا عليهن سبيلا ـ الاهل بلغت ؟ اللهم فاشهد ـ

يا ايها الناس ! اسمعوا و اطيعوا و ان امر عليكم عبد جشى مجدع اقام فيكم كتاب الله ـ

ايها الناس ! ان الله قدادى الى كل ذى حق حقه ـ ولا تجوز وصية لوارث ـ ولا تجوز وصية فى اكثر من الثلث ـ

والولد للفراش، و للعاهر الحجر ـ و من ادعى الى غيرابيه او تولى غير مواليه فعليه لعنة الله والملائكة و الناس اجمعين ـ لا يقبل الله منه صرفا و عدلا ـ

ايها الناس ! ان الشيطان قديئس ان يعبد فى ارضكم هذه ابدا ـ ولكنه رضى ان يطاع فيما سوى ذلك مما تحقرون من اعمالكم فاحذروه على دينكم ـ

"Behold, receive with kindness the recommendation given about women. For they are middle-aged women (or helpers) with you. They do not possess anything for themselves and you cannot have from them more than that. If they obey you in this way, then you should not treat them unjustly   Lo. have I conveyed? O Allah, be witness.

O, people, listen and obey though a mangled Abyssinian slave becomes your Amir who executes the Book of Allah among you.

"O people, verily Allah appropriated to every one his due. No will is valid for an inheritor and a will is not lawful for more than one-third (of the property).

"The child belongs to the (legal) bed and for the adulterer there is stoning. He who relates (his genealogy) to other than his father or claims his clientship to other than his masters, the curse of Allah, the angels and the people--all these--be upon him. Allah will accept from him neither repentance nor righteousness.

"O people, verily the Satan is disappointed from being ever worshipped in this land of yours. But he is satisfied to be obeyed in other than that you think very trifling of your actions. So be cautious of him in your religion."

فانى قد تركت فيكم ما ان اخذ تم به لن تضلوا بعده—امرآ ابينا ۔
كتاب الله و سنة رسوله ۔

يا معشر الناس ! اتانى جبرئيل ، فا قرانى من ربى السلام و قال :
ان الله غفر لا هل عرفات و اهل المشعر و ضمن عنهم التبعات ۔

"Verily, I have left behind among you that which
if you catch hold of you will never be misled later on--
a conspicuous thing, *i.e.*, the Book of Allah and *Sunnat*
of His Apostle.

"O people, Jibra'il (Gabriel) came to me, conveyed
salam from my Lord and said; Verily Allah has forgiven
the people of 'Arafat and the Sanctuary and stood a
guarantee for (forgoing) their shortcomings."

فقام عمر بن الخطاب فقال : يا رسول الله ! هذا لنا خاصة ؟ قال :
هذا لكم و لمن اتى بعد كم الى يوم القيامة ـ
و انتم تسئلون عنى، فما انتم قائلون ؟ قالوا : نشهد انك قدبلغت،
و اديت و نصحت ـ
فقال باصبعه السبابة ير فعها الى السماء وينكتها الى الناس : اللهم
اشهد، اللهم اشهد، اللهم اشهد ـ

'Umar--binu'l--Khattab stood up and said: "O
Apostle of Allah, is it for us only?" He replied: "It
is for you and for those who are to come after you
till the Day of Resurrection.

"And you will be asked about me, then what
would you say?" They replied: "We bear witness that
you have conveyed the message, discharged (your duty)
and admonished."

Then he said raising his ring-finger towards
heaven and pointing it out towards the people: "O Allah,
bear witness; O Allah, bear witness; O Allah, bear

witness."[1]

No. 25--*The following oration was delivered by the Holy Prophet during his Farewell Pilgrimage at Mina on Friday, 10th Dhu'l-Hijjah, 10 A.H. before the sun fall.*

حمد الله و اثنى عليه ثم قال : يا ايها الناس ! اسمعوا قولى فانى لا اذرى، لعلى لا القا كم بعد عامى هذا بهذا الموقف ابدا ـ

يا ايها الناس ! انما النسئى زيادة فى الكفر ـ يضل به الذين كفروا ـ يحلونه عاما ، و يحر مونه عاما ليوا طئوا عدة ما حرم الله، فيحلوا ما حرم الله (القران سورة التوبة) و يحرموا ما احل الله ـ

ان الزمان قد استدار كهيئته يوم خلق السموات و الارض ـ و ان عدة الشهور عناء الله اثنا عشر شهرا ـ منها اربعة حرم ـ ثلث متواليات : ذوالقعدة و ذوالحجة و المحرم و رجب مضر الذى بين جمادى و شعبان ـ

ايها الناس ! هل تدرون اى يوم هذا ؟ قالوا : الله ورسوله اعلم ـ فسكت حتى ظننا انه سيسميه بغير اسمه ـ فقال : اليس يوم النحر ؟ قلنا : بلى يا رسول الله !

He praised Allah, thanked Him and said: "O people, listen to my words; verily I do not know, I may not ever meet you after my this year at this place.

---

1. Mishkat (Delhi ed.) p. 224; Muslim, Farewell Pilgrimage; Ibn Hisham, Vol. II, pp. 389, 391; Tirmidhi, (Lucknow ed.)., pp. 315, 440; Tafsir, Anfar; Ibn Sa'd, Vol. II, Pt. 1, p. 132; Bayun, Vol. II p. 24; Targhib (ed. Egypt), Vol. II, p. 75.

"O people, verily the intercalation (of a prohibited month) is only an addition to infidelity. Thereby the unbelievers are led to wrong. For they make it lawful one year and forbidden in another year to be in conformity with the number (of months) which Allah declared unlawful so they consider violable what Allah declared inviolable (Q. ix 37) and they consider inviolable what Allah declared violable.

"Verily the time has revolved just as in its own from (way) from the day of the creation of heavens and the earth. The number of months to Allah is twelve of which four are sacred; three are consecutive--Dhu'l-Qa'dah, Dhu'l-Hijjah and Muharram; and Rajabu Mudar which is between Jumada and Sha'ban.

"O people, do you know what Day it is? They said: "Allah and His Apostle know the best." He remained silent till we thought that he would call it by another name. Then he said: "Is it not the Day of Sacrifice? We said: "Yes, O Apostle of Allah."

فقال : اى شهر هذا ؟ قلنا : الله و رسوله اعلم ـ فسكت حتى ظننا
انه سيسميه بغير اسمه ـ قال : اليس ذوالحجة ؟ قلنا : بلى ـ

قال : اى بلد هذا ؟ قلنا : الله و رسوله اعلم ـ فسكت حتى ظننا
انه سيسميه بغير اسمه ـ فقال : اليست ببلدة الحرام ؟ قلنا : بلى '
يا رسول الله ـ

قال : فان دماء كم و اسوالكم و اعراضكم و ابشار كم عليكم
حرام كحرمة يومكم هذا فى شهر كم هذا فى بلد كم هذا ـ الا هل بلغت ؟
اللهم اشهد ـ

الا لا يجنى جان الا على نفسه ـ ولا يجنى والد على ولده ولا ولد
على والده ـ

الا ان المسلم اخوالمسلم ـ فلا يحل لامرئ من اخيه الا ما اعطاه
عن طيب نفس منه ـ فلا تظلمن انفسكم ـ اللهم هل بلغت ؟

Then he asked: "What month is it? We replied:
"Allah and His Apostle know the best". He remained
silent till we thought that he would name it with another
name. Then he said: "Is it not the month of Dhu'l-
Hijjah?" We said: "Yes".

He said: "What city is it?" We said: "Allah and
His Apostle know the best." He remained silent till
we thought that he would give it another name. Then
he said: "Is it not the Sacred City?" We replied: "Yes,
O Apostle of Allah."

He said: "So verily your blood (lives), your
properties, your honour and your skins are sacred and
inviolable to yourselves just as the sacredness of this
your Day in this your Month in this City." Lo, have
I conveyed? O Allah ! bear witness.

"Behold, no criminal committing a crime is
responsible for it but himself. No son is responsible
for the crime of his father and no father is responsible
for the crime of his son."

Behold, the Muslim is the brother of the Muslim.
So nothing is lawful for a man from his brother except
what he gives him willingly. So you should not oppress
yourselves. O Allah! have I conveyed?"

ان الله قد قسم لكل انسان نصيبه من الميراث ـ فلا تجوز لوارث
وصية ـ الاوان الولد للفراش و للعاصر الحجر ـ
الا و من ادعى الى غير ابيه اوتولى غير مواليا رغبة عنهم فعليه
لعنة الله و الملائكة و الناس اجمعين ـ
ارقاء كم ؟ ارقاء كم ـ اطعموهم مما تاكلون ـ و البسوهم مما
تلبسون ـ
و ان جاؤوا بذنب لا تريدون ان تغفروه فبيعوا عباد الله، ولا
تعذ بوهم
يا ايها الناس ! اتقوا الله، و ان امر عليكم عبد حبشى مجدع
فاسمعوا له و اطيعوا ما اقام لكم كتاب الله ـ

"Verily, Allah has allotted for every man his lot of inheritance. So no will is lawful for an inheritor. Behold, verily the child belongs to the (legal) bed, and the adulterer is to be stoned.

"Behold, he who claims (his genealogy) to other than his father or traces his clientship to other than his masters disliking them, upon him be curse of Allah, the angels and the people--all these.

"Take care of your slaves; take care of your slaves. Feed them from what eat and clothe them from what you wear.

"If they commit any crime which you do not like to forgive, then sell the bonds of Allah and do not chastise them.

"O people, fear Allah; and (even) if a mangled Abyssinian slave becomes your chief hearken to him and obey as long as he executes the Book of Allah."

الا تسمعون، اعبدوا ربكم ـ و صلوا خمسكم ـ و صوموا شهركم ـ و حجوا بيتكم ـ و ادوا زكوة اموالكم طيبة انفسكم ـ و اطيعوا اذا امرتكم ـ تدخلوا جنة ربكم ـ

و انكم ستلقون ربكم ـ فيسئلكم عن اعمالكم ـ الا فلا ترجعوا بعدى ضلا لا يضرب بعضكم رقاب بعض ـ الا هل بلغت ؟ قالوا : نعم ـ قال : اللهم اشهد ـ

الا فليبلغ الشاهد الـ ائب ـ فانه رب مبلغ اوعى من سامع ـ

"Behold do hear me. Worship your Lord; pray your five times; fast your month; make pilgrimage of your House (Ka'ba); pay willingly the fixed poor-rate of your property and obey when (and what) I command you; (then) you will enter the Heaven of your Lord.

"Verily you will soon meet your Lord. So He will ask you about your actions. Behold, do not go astray after me so that some of you strike the neck of others. Lo, have I conveyed the message?" They said: "Yes." He said: "O Allah, bear witness.

"Lo, let the present ones convey the message to the absent ones. For verily many people to whom the message is conveyed may be more mindful of it than the audience."[1] (see next page)

No. 26--*The following oration was delivered by the Holy Prophet at Mina during his Farewell Pilgrimage on 11 or 12 Dhu'l-Hijjah, 10. A.H.*

فحمد الله واثنى عليه ـ ثم ذكر المسيح الدجال ـ فاظنب فى ذكره
و قال : مابعث الله من نبى الا انذر امته ـ انذره نوح و النبيون من
بعده ـ و انه يخرج فيكم ـ فما خفى عليكم من شانه ـ فليس يخفى عليكم
ان ربكم ليس باعور و انه اعور عين اليمنى ـ كان عينه عنبة طافية ـ

ايها الناس ! ان ربكم واحد ـ و اباكم واحد ـ كلكم لادم ـ وادم
من تراب ـ الا لا فضل لعربى على عجمى ولا لعجمى على عربى ـ ولا
لا حمر على اسود، ولا لاسود على احمر الا بالتقوى ـ ان اكرمكم عند
الله اتقا كم ـ

الا هل بعلت ؟ قالوا : بلى، يا رسول الله ! قال : فليبلغ الشاهد
الغائب ـ

الا اتدرون اى يوم هذا ؟ قالو : الله و رسوله اعلم ـ
قال : هذا وسط ايام التشريق ـ

قال : تدرون اى بلد هذا ؟ قالوا : الله و رسوله اعلم ـ قال : هذا
المشعر الحرام ـ

ثم قال : انى لا ادرى، لعلى لا القاكم بعد هذا ـ الا وان دماءكم
واموالكم واعراضكم عليكم حرام كحرمة يومكم هذا، فى بلد كم هذا،
حتى تلقوا ربكم ـ فيسلكم هن اعمالكم ـ

الا فيبلغ اد ناكم اقصاكم ـ الا هل بلغت ؟

---

1. Bukhari, pp 236, 833, 1048; Muslim, Farewell Pilgrimage; Tirmidhi,
(ed. Lucknow), p. 315; Tahrimud-Dimai Wal-Amwal. 440; Tafsir Ibn
Hisham, Vol. II, pp. 389, 391. Farewell Pilgrimage; Ibn Sa'd, Vol. III,
Pt. I.P. 285; Zad, Vol. I, pp. 228-245; Muntakhab (ed. Hyderabad),
Vol. I P. 9. Kitab I, Iman.

He praised Allah and thanked Him; then he mentioned the Messiah, the Dajjal (Anti-Christ) and made a long description of him and said: "Allah did not send any Prophet but he warned his followers. Noah and the Prophets after him cautioned of him. The fact is that he will appear among you . There may be something of his condition hidden from you, but it can never be concealed to you that your Lord is not one-eyed while he is devoid of the right eye and as if it is a rotten grape.

"O people, verily your Lord is one and your father is one. All of you belong to Adam and Adam is (made) of earth. Behold, there is no superiority for an Arab over a non-Arab and for a non-Arab: over an Arab; nor for a red coloured over a black- coloured and for a black skinned over a red-skinned except in piety. Verily the noblest among you is he who is the most pious.

"Lo, have I conveyed?" They said "Yes, O Apostle of Allah." He said: "Let the present ones convey the message to the absent ones.

"Lo, do you know what day it is ?" They answered: Allah and His Apostle know the best."

He said: "It is the middle of the days of Tashriq (desiccation of meat in the sun)."

He enquired: "Do you know what city it is?" They replied: "Allah and His Apostle know the best." He said: "It is the sacred Mash'ar (the place of the ritual of the Pilgrimage)."

Then he said: "Verily I do not know whether I shall meet you hereafter. Behold, you lives, your properties and your honour are, indeed, sacred and inviolable just as the sanctity of this your day in this your city till you meet your Lord. Then He will ask you about your actions."

"Behold, the nearer ones of you should convey the message to the remoter ones. Lo, have I conveyed the message?"

No. 27--*The following oration was delivered by the Holy Prophet at a watery place called Khumm on his way from Makkah to Madina in 10 A.H.*

فحمد الله واثنى عليه و وعظ و ذكر، ثم قال : اما بعد، الا ايها الناس ! فانما انابشر يوشك ان ياتى رسول ربى ــ فاجيب ــ

وانا تارك فيكم ثقلين : أولهما كتاب الله ــ فيه الهدى والنور ــ فخذوا بكتاب الله واستمسكوا به ٠٠٠٠ واهل بيتى ــ أذكركم الله فى اهل بيتى ــ اذكركم الله فى اهل بيتى ــ اذكركم الله فى اهل بيتى ــ

He praised Allah, thanked Him, admonished and exhorted, and then he said: "Now to proceed, be aware, O people, I am nothing but a human being; the messenger of my Lord is about to come and accordingly I shall have to respond.

"I would leave behind among you two important things: The first of them is the Book of Allah which contains guidance and light. So take the Book of Allah and grasp it.... And (the second is) my family, I remind

you, by Allah of my family. I remind you by Allah, of my
family. I remind you by Allah, of my family."[1]

No. 28--*The following oration was delivered by the
Holy Prophet on Monday, the 26th Safar, 11 A.H.*

صعد المنبر فحمد الله و اثنى عليه، ثم قال : امابعد، ايها الناس !
فما مقالة بلغتنى عن بعضكم فى تأ ميرى اسامة ؟

ولئن طعنتم فى تاميرى أسامة لقد طعنتم فى امارق اباه من قبله ـ
و ايم الله ، ان كان للامارة لخليقا ، وانه كان لا حب الناس الى ـ
وان ابنه هذا من بعده لخليق للا مارة ـ وان كان لا حب الناس
الى ـ وانهما لمخيلان لكل خير ـ فاستو صوا به خيرا ـ فانه من خيارگم ـ

He mounted the pulpit, praised Allah and thanked
Him and then he said: "As for next, O people, what
is this that has reached me from some of you
concerning my appointing Usama to the post of a
commander?"

"If you have, indeed, criticised my appointing
Usama as *Amir*, (it is not a new thing, for) you have,
indeed criticised my appointing his father (Zaid) as
Amir before him. By Allah, he (Zaid) was undoubtedly
the fit man for being appointed as *Amir* and he was
surely the most beloved person to me."

"After him this son of his is, indeed, a fit man for

commandership and he is, undoubtedly one of the most
beloved persons to me. They both are, indeed, apt to
do good. So you welcome him as the best one; for he
is among your best ones."[1]

No. 29--*Just five days before death during his last
illness with a greasy bandage on his head and a
wrapper on his shoulder, inclining to the shoulders of
'Ali and Fadl, the Holy Prophet came out from 'Ai'shah's
room to the mosque, sat on the first step of the pulpit
and delivered his last oration. It was Thursday, the 8th
of Rabi-ul-Awwal, 11 A.H. according to Shibli Nu'mani,
(Sirat-un-Nabi).*

فحمد الله و اثنى عليه واستغفر للشهداء من أصحاب احد و دعا لهم
ثم قال : ايها الناس ! الى ـ فثابو اليه ـ.

ثم قال : امابعد، ان رجلا خيره ربه بين ان يعيش فى الدنيا ماشاء
ان يعيش ويأ كل من الدنيا ماشاء ان يأ كل وبين لقاء ربه ـ

فبكى ابوبكر، و قال : بل نفديك باباثنا و امهاتنا واموالنا ٠٠٠
٠٠٠٠ فقال رسول الله صلى الله عليه وسلم : ما من احد امن الينا فى
صحبته و ماله من ابن ابى قحافة ـ ولوكنت متخذا خليلا غير ربى لا
تخذت ابن ابى قحافة خليلا ـ ولكن ود واخاء ايمان ـ مرتين اوثلثا ـ
و ان صاحبكم خليل الله ـ لا يبقين فى المسجد باب الا باب ابى
بكر ـ

He praised Allah, thanked Him, sought
forgiveness for the martyrs of the battle of Uhad and

1.Ibn Sa'd, Vol. II, Pt. I, PP. 41, 136

prayed for them. Then he said: "O people, (draw near) to me. " So they gathered round him.

Then he said: "Well, there is a man whose Lord has given him option between living in this world as long as he wishes to live and eating from this world as much as he likes to eat, or meeting his Lord."

(Hearing it) Abu Bakr wept and said: "Nay, may our fathers, mothers and properties be your ransom..."

Then the Apostle of Allah--may Allah send him bliss and peace!--said: "There is none more bountiful to us for his company and wealth than the son of Abu Quhafa (Abu Bakr). Had I taken my intimate friend except my Lord, I would have taken the son of Abu Quhafah as my intimate friend. But there is love and brotherhood of Faith"- He said it (twice or thrice).

"The fact is that your companion is the intimate friend of Allah. There should not remain in the mosque any door (open) except the door of Abu Bakr."

يا ايها الناس ! بلغنى انكم تخافون من موت نبيكم - هل خلد نبى قبلى فى من بعث اليه ، فاخلد فيكم ؟

الا انى لا حق بربى - وانكم لا حقوق به - فا و صيكم بالمهاجرين الاولين ـ و اوصى المهاجرين فيما بينهم -

فان الله تعالى يقول : والعصر - ان الانسان لفى خسر ـ الى اخرها ـ

وان الامور تجرى باذن الله تعالى - ولا يحملنكم استبطاء امر على استعجاله - فان الله عز وجل لا يعجل بعجلة احد -

ومن غالب الله غلبه ـ و من خادع الله خدعه ـ فهل عسيتم ان
تو ليتم ان تفسدوا فى الارض و تقطعوا ارحامكم ـ
و اوصيكم بالانصار خيرا ـ فانهم الذين تبوؤوا الدار و الايمان من
قبلكم ـ ان تحسنوا اليهم ـ
الم يشاطر و كم فى الثمار ؟ الم يوسعوا لكم فى الدار ؟ الم
يؤثر و كم على انفسهم و بهم الخصامة ؟

"O people, it has reached me that you are afraid
of your Prophet's death. Has any previous prophet lived
for ever among those to whom he was sent: so that I
would live for ever among you?

"Behold, I am going to my Lord and you will be
going to Him. I recommend you to do good to the First
Emigrants and I recommend the Emigrants to do good
among themselves.

"Lo, Allah, the Exalted, says: 'By the time, Man
is in loss'--to the end of the Sura (ciii).

"Verily the things run with the permission of Allah,
the Exalted, and verily delay in a matter should not urge
you on its hastening in demand. Allah,--the Mighty and
the Great--does not hasten for the hastiness of anybody.

"He who contends with Allah, He overcomes him.
He who tries to deceive Allah, He outwits him. In
a near future if you get the authority then do no

mischief on the earth and do not cut off your blood
relations.

"I recommended you to do good to the helpers.
They are those who prepared the lodging and faith
for you. So you should behave them well.

"Did they not divide with you their fruits equally?
Did they not make space for you in their houses? Did
they not prefer you to themselves houses? Did they not
prefer you to themselves while poverty was with them?'

الافان الناس يكثرون ـ وتقل الانصار ـ حتى يكونوا فى الناس بمنزلة
الملح فى الطعام - هم عيبتى التى آويت اليها ـ و نعلى، و كرشى التى
اكل فيها ـ فاحفظونى فيهم ـ

والذى نفسى بيده ، انى لا حبكم، ان الانصار قد قضوا ما عليهم ـ
و بقى ما عليكم ـ

فمن ولى منكم شيأ فاستطاع ان يضر فيه قوما او ينفع فيه اخرين،
فليقبل من محسنهم و يتجاوز عن مسيئهم - الا ولا تستأ ثروا عليهم ـ
.. و انى فرط لكم ـ و انا شهيد عليكم ـ وانتم لا حقون بى ـ الا
وان موعدكم الحوض- وانى و الله لا نظر الى حوضى الان من مقامى هذا ـ
الا، من احب ان يرده على غدا فليكف يده ولسانه الا فيما ينبغى ـ

"Lo, men will increase in number, but the helpers
will decrease to the extent that they will be among men
as salt in food. They are my family with whom I took
my shelter; they are my sandals; and they are my
paunch in which I eat. So observe me in them.

"By Him in Whose hand is my life, verily I love you; verily the helpers have done what was on them and there remains what is on you.

"So he who from among you gets power in any matter and becomes able to do harm to people therein or to do good to other therein, then he should appreciate one of them who does well and should overlook one of them who does bad. Lo, do not be selfish about them.

"Behold, I shall precede you; I will be your witness and you are to meet me. Lo, the 'Haud' is your meeting place. By Allah, just now, I see my 'haud' from here.

"Beware, he who likes to come to it along with me tomorrow, should hold back his hand and tongue except from necessary matters."

وانى قد اعطيت مفاتيح خزائن الارض ـ وانى والله ما اخاف عليكم
ان تشركوا بعدى ـ و لكنى اخاف عليكم ان تنافسوا فيها فتقتتلوا
فتهلكوا كما هلك من كان قبلكم ـ

يا ايها الناس ! ان الذنوب تغير النعم و تبدل القسم فاذابر الناس
بربهم اعتهم واذا فجر الناس عقوهم ـ

"Lo, I have, indeed, been given the keys of the treasures of the earth. By Allah, I do not fear for you that you will turn polytheists after me. But I fear for you that you will be entangled in them, then you will fight one another and will perish like those who perished before you.

"O people, verily the sins spoil the blessings and change the lots. When the people are good, their rulers do good to them and when the people are bad, they oppress them."

ثم قال : انه قد دنامنى حقوق من بين اظهر كم و انما انا بشر ـ
فايما رجل كنت اصبت من عرضه شيئاً فهذا عرضى ، فليقتص ـ
و ايما رجل كنت اصبت من بشره شيئاً ـ فهذا بشرى ، فليقتص ـ
وايما رجل كنت اصبت من ماله شيئاً فهذا مالى، فليأ خذ ـ واعلموا
ان او لا كم بى رجل كان له من ذلك شيئى، فاخذه او حللنى فلقيت ربى
و انا محلل لى ـ

ولا يقولن رجل انى اخاف العداوة والشحناء من رسول الله ـ فانهما
ليستا من طبيعتى ولا من خلقى ؛ ومن غلبته نفسه على شيئى فليستعن بى
حتى ادعوله ـ

"Then he said: "There may be some rights which I owe to you and I am nothing but a human being. So if there be any man whose honour I have injured a bit, here is my honour! he may retaliate.

"Whosoever he may be if I have wounded a bit of his skin, here is my skin; He may retaliate.

"Whosoever he may be, if I have taken anything from his property, here is my property; so he may take. Know that he, among you, is more loyal to me who has got such a thing and takes it or absolves me; then I meet my Lord while I am absolved.

"Nobody should say, I fear enmity and grudge of the Apostle of Allah. Verily these things are not in my